FOUL DEEDS AND SUSPICIOUS DEATHS AROUND NORTHAMPTON

TRUE CRIME FROM WHARNCLIFFE

Foul Deeds and Suspicious Deaths Series

Staffordshire and the Potteries
Colchester
Manchester
Guilford
Derby
Northampton
Pontefract and Castleford
Tees
Bedford
Bristol
Carlisle
Newcastle
Southend-on-Sea
Barnsley
Birmingham
Blackburn and Hyndburn
Chesterfield
Coventry
Ealing
Guernsey
Huddersfield
Leeds
Liverpool
Newport
Nottingham
Rotherham
London East End
Wigan

More Foul Deeds Wakefield
Mansfield
Leicester
Stratford and South Warwickshire
Brighton
Folkestone and Dover
Oxfordshire
Black Country
Durham
Bradford
Cambridge
Halifax
Scunthorpe
Barking, Dagenham & Chadwell Heath
Bath
More Foul Deeds Birmingham
Bolton
More Foul Deeds Chesterfield
Croydon
Grimsby
Hampstead, Holborn and St Pancras
Hull
Lewisham and Deptford
London's West End
Norfolk
Portsmouth
Warwickshire
York

OTHER TRUE CRIME BOOKS FROM WHARNCLIFFE

Norfolk Mayhem and Murder
The A-Z of London Murders
Unsolved Murders in Victorian &
Edwardian London
Unsolved Yorkshire Murders
A-Z Yorkshire Murder
Brighton Crime and Vice 1800-2000
Essex Murders

Executions & Hangings in Newcastle
and Morpeth
Norwich Murders
Unsolved Norfolk Murders
Yorkshire's Murderous Women
Black Barnsley
Durham Executions
Strangeways Hanged

Please contact us via any of the methods below for more information
or a catalogue.

WHARNCLIFFE BOOKS

47 Church Street – Barnsley – South Yorkshire – S70 2AS
Tel: 01226 734555 – 734222 Fax: 01226 734438
E-mail: enquiries@pen-and-sword.co.uk
Website: www.wharncliffebooks.co.uk

Foul Deeds and Suspicious Deaths Around
Northampton

PAUL HARRISON

Series Editor
Brian Elliott

Wharncliffe Books

First Published in Great Britain in 2007 by
Wharncliffe Books
an imprint of
Pen and Sword Books Limited,
47 Church Street, Barnsley,
South Yorkshire. S70 2AS

Copyright © Paul Harrison, 2007

All illustrations are from the Author's collection

ISBN: 978 1 845630 35 5

A CIP catalogue record of this book is available from the
British Library

Typeset in Plantin and Benguiat by
Pen and Sword Books Ltd

Printed in the United Kingdom by
Biddles Ltd

Pen & Sword Books Ltd incorporates the imprints of
Pen & Sword Aviation, Pen & Sword Maritime,
Pen & Sword Military, Wharncliffe Local History, Pen & Sword Select,
Pen & Sword Military Classics and Leo Cooper.

For a complete list of Pen & Sword titles please contact:
PEN & SWORD BOOKS LIMITED
47 Church Street, Barnsley, South Yorkshire, S70 2AS, England.
E-mail: enquiries@pen-and-sword.co.uk
Website: www.pen-and-sword.co.uk

Contents

Dedication

For the most wonderful and beautiful grandchildren
any grandfather could wish for, Mia and Thomas Robinson

Acknowledgements

I t is often left unsaid by authors that the contents of a published book are actually crafted by many: the author is merely the storyteller, a wordsmith. Without doubt this work is the product of a genuine collective effort, gathered, developed and researched over a period of fifteen years, not least from the primary members of the Harrison family, including my good companion, Bingo, who is a wonderful Belgian shepherd rescue dog, complete with attitude!

I would like to give my sincere appreciation to the following individuals and organisations for their help and support. Special praise goes to my mentor and literary role model, Jonathan Goodman, who has been a huge source of inspiration to me over the last decade or so. To the dedicated staff of the county library services, particularly those in Kettering and Northampton, who greatly aided my research by identifying and locating old and often difficult to find documents and newspapers. To the late Albert Morby, of Burton Latimer, a truly fine man and ambassador for the area, thank you for everything you did for me, my old friend – you were more of an inspiration than you probably knew or realised. To the late Dame Miriam Lane, who unwittingly and therefore unintentionally inspired my research into the hitherto unsolved Ashton murder case, by giving me a unique lead as to who the chief suspect was at the time of the killings. To Alf Brown, another true gentleman, who was, of course, a leading witness in the case against Alfred Arthur Rouse. Over the years I spent many hours with Alf at his Northampton home, talking mostly, of course, about the Rouse case, but also of Northampton life as he recalled it. I dread to think how much of Alf's wonderful tea we consumed during such sessions. In addition to this I would like to place on record my sincere appreciation and praise of Dom Addicott; surely no person knows more about the history of the village of Hardingstone than he. To Norman and the Wilsden family for aiding me with the facts surrounding the potential identity of Rouse's unknown victim.

To BBC Radio Northampton, and in particular, Dave Watkins, who in those early days actually gave me direction with my book writing. He provided me with my very first 'airing' and offered the advice which I followed; a true inspiration. Also at BBC Radio Northampton, I can't forget the wonderful Anna Murby for her serious support (over countless – really too many – years) of my research, interviewing me time and again about such subjects as Jack the Ripper, murder and mysteries from the county and, in the late-1990s, about the enduring mystery of the Loch Ness monster! To David O' Dowd, a former Chief Constable of Northamptonshire Police, for allowing me formal access to official files on many of the cases contained herein, and who positively urged me to record in book format the county's hitherto hidden history. A big thank you to a good and true friend, Andy Hall MBE, potentially Carlisle United's greatest supporter, whose proactive encouragement to all my writing has been gratefully appreciated. Cheers, mate.

As sad as it seems, I want to make mention of my beloved computer, without which I would be absolutely lost. Finally, and most importantly, I would like to say a huge thank you to everyone who took the time to write or to telephone me, willing me to pursue another volume covering the foul deeds of the county. For all of you, here it is – I sincerely hope you find it more enjoyable than the first volume. I have found this most current volume to be utterly captivating, not only while carrying out the further research and writing down the updates and further graphic detail omitted from the original, first volume, but when reading through the completed manuscript.

Paul Harrison
December 2006

Introduction

Since the unrivalled local success of my first book, *Northamptonshire Murders*, way back in 1991, I have received on average two letters a week from correspondents wishing to discuss with me all matters regarding the deadly criminous in one of Britain's most beautiful counties, Northamptonshire. The interest that particular book aroused and generated was for me somewhat overwhelming; it bred discussions on radio shows and television documentaries, both locally and nationally. It provided me with opportunities to discuss the hidden side to Northamptonshire history at public events and at society events. It provided me with so much more information, facts and stories that I didn't know of. Similarly, there can be no doubting the fact that it also inspired other would-be researchers and authors to try to emulate that success. A number have attempted to follow the same route, but the majority have failed to capture the emotive reality of crimes such as murder and how it grips and affects entire communities, even nations.

So when I approached Wharncliffe Books with the idea of this project, *Foul Deeds and Suspicious Deaths Around Northampton*, I very much wanted to project my enthusiasm to record what the very title of this work indicates. This volume is, I believe, the definitive version of all such matters relating to county of Northamptonshire.

I can say in all honesty that, no matter where one travels in the county, one is never too far from the county town of Northampton, filled with a celebrated history of boot- and shoe-making. The Battle of Naseby also took place in the county boundaries in 1645, and then there was a great fire in 1675 which destroyed a massive amount of property.

Such is the often-untouched tranquil beauty of the county that it is still possible to this day to find many of the historical sites identified in this work. Meandering meadows and picturesque countryside are to be found in abundance; canals, rivers and peace and serenity are as evident now as they were many centuries ago. Little wonder then, that the county is referred to as the Rose of the Shires. Fotheringhay

Church, for example, has to be one of the most photographed and picture-published churches worldwide, yet few know that this is where two of the murder victims from a tale contained in this work are buried. It is also extremely close to the place of execution of Mary Queen of Scots – Fotheringhay Castle.

Behind this glowing testimony, which refers solely to the beauty of the county, sits, somewhat uncomfortably, a more sinister side to the history of the area that I hope this book encapsulates. A sinister world which, for example, encompasses the practice of witchcraft, and the visits to the county by the Witchfinder General himself, Matthew Hopkins, and his cronies in 1645 and 1646 respectively, the details of which have not been recorded locally before. In the majority of cases a visit from the Witchfinder General meant certain death for those who were deemed different or led a quiet existence away from village intimacy. Then there is the act of murder: there can be no doubting the fact that Hopkins was as guilty of murder as any murder suspect named in this book, yet he somehow evaded justice, instead dying from consumption in rural Essex. It is suggested that Hopkins was responsible for the deaths of at least two hundred people he wrongly accused of being witches in a two-year reign of terror.

Hidden away among the once dusty archives in Northampton County Record Office is a wealth of material which records murder and mayhem across the county, including witchcraft, and murder for all manner of reasons. In the two-volume set of *Chronicles of Crime*, published in 1841, even more sinister matters are recorded. These, then, have been the main focal points of my research. During my journey I have taken nothing for granted; I have reviewed so-called facts and further researched many of the 'better-known' crimes, resulting in exciting intrigue and unearthing further mysteries.

This work, while not a complete record of suspicious circumstances throughout the county, provides a real flavour of some of the foulest deeds to have occurred. There can be no denying that, no matter which way you look at it or may try to disguise it, Northampton and its surrounding areas have a sinister and criminal past to match any other county the length and breadth of the British Isles.

Chapter 1

A Miscellany of Murder
1291-1897

*A brief tour of some of the earlier historical murders
to occur in and around Northampton. Sometimes
gruesome and often sadistic, but always gripping.*

T he history of murderous activity in the county is littered with older cases, detailed information of which is sparse. The following few stories are just a small sample of those which cannot be more specifically discussed or of which very little more information is known.

The case of Martin of Littlebury is hardly one which conjures images of an evil and reckless killer. Yet in the space of thirty-two years Martin was involved in three individual killings. Each time, through his cunning and devious manner, he escaped justice. According to what records remain extant, he first committed the act of murder one night in 1291. It seems that he met with Geoffrey, the son of Alexander Broun of Bradden, on the banks of the Cherwell at a place called 'le Mede' in Chipping Warden. There is no record of animosity between the pair, but it seems that they were clearly enemies. Martin fired an arrow from his bow at Geoffrey. The arrow took down and killed its intended target instantly. Realising what he had done, Martin made good his escape but was later captured and subsequently incarcerated in Northampton Castle, where he awaited trial.

At the trial that followed, it was revealed that he killed the man in an act of self-defence. It should be borne in mind that in the thirteenth century, taking a life through force was essentially murder. There were no grounds for diminished responsibilities or defences to the finality of the act. Murder was murder, end of story. Martin was therefore guilty of murder and held in custody while awaiting sentencing. During this period he escaped, and remained at large until 1305.

Nothing else was heard of the man until Wednesday, 8 September 1305, when he killed the parish priest of Woodford Halse, William de Hynton. There is no recorded reason or motive for this act, but once again, Martin made his way from the murder scene with a clear plan of action to escape justice. He made his way to the sanctuary of Chipping Warden church. Here he confessed to the crime and abjured (was banished from) the realm as opposed to being executed for the crime.

Eighteen years later, in 1323, Martin once again returned to haunt the county. Returning to Chipping Warden, he announced that he had a king's pardon, which therefore allowed him to be in the country. This displeased many people who knew he was a brutal and calculated killer and miscreant. During this brief period he was involved in many a fracas. During one such confrontation he deliberately stabbed one Geoffrey of Warden through the heart, killing him instantly. Martin went into hiding yet again and managed to escape justice. Fortunately, in Northampton, anyway, nothing more was ever heard of the sinister activity of this killer.

The murder of the mock vicar Theophilus Hart in 1685 would, in all likelihood have made the front page headlines of every Sunday tabloid had it occurred in more recent times. Theophilus Hart was little more than a conman. Sophisticated in his use of people in power to profit his own personal status, he had, through his gentrified contacts, managed to install himself as vicar of Wappenham and, a short time later, Blakesley. This ensured that he received two salaries for providing cover to two villages.

As can be seen, Hart was anything but a decent and honest vicar: he did what was necessary to enhance his own position either materialistically or through the sins of the flesh. He had a reputation locally as something of a womaniser and there were apparently many rumours circulating about whom he was sleeping with.

So it was that on Tuesday, 23 January 1685, the local butcher to Wappenham, George Tarry, visited Wappenham rectory. There is some reason to believe that rumours had confirmed to him his deepest suspicions, first aroused by his wife's recent change in attitude, that she was being unfaithful to him. Arriving at the house, he let himself in through the open front door. He could hear voices upstairs and quietly ascended the staircase. Moving swiftly, he burst into the bedroom where the noises came from. There his suspicions were confirmed and he found his wife in bed with Hart. The couple were shocked by the intrusion, and the mock vicar, realising that danger lay ahead, apologised profusely and begged for forgiveness. Callously, he blamed the butcher's wife for leading him on and throwing herself at him! He then made a dash for it, running naked down the stairs, out of the house and into the nearby fields. Without being too dismissive of the situation, it must have looked like a scene from a farce. Close behind the naked 65-year-old was the angry and volatile butcher, who carried with him butchers' tools. Soon he caught up with the fleeing man and battered him to the ground. The vicar, helpless again, pleaded for mercy, but his cries were futile. The butcher, a skilled craftsman, duly removed his brains from his skull and left them alongside the body. A more fitting and gruesome end to the activities of a dastardly criminal I cannot think of.

George Tarry made no secret of what he had done and why he had done it. He was charged with, and found guilty of, murder. At the

The County Gaol, where George Tarry was held in 1685. Northants Record Office

resulting trial, his defence was based on the infidelity of his wife and the unethical actions of Theophilus Hart. The jury would have none of it: he was hanged at Northampton on Tuesday, 27 May 1685 before an extremely large and hostile crowd.

Isaac Pinnock was a nineteen-year-old boy who lived in Rothwell. He was, to put it mildly, regarded as a troublemaker and a damned nuisance around the town. He was prone to unnecessary acts of vandalism, breaking windows, damaging street furniture such as flowerpots, and for generally causing much trouble among the town's residents. He was also prone to committing wanton and mindless violence on his younger peers, bullying them for meagre possessions such as sweets or a few pennies.

Locally he had earned himself a reputation as a problem. It seems that no one liked his attitude and as a result he was alienated by the society. This in turn caused him to commit greater acts of vandalism and crime to attract attention to himself. At one point, he stole a ewe and a lamb from a local man, Ben Cheney, for no purpose other than to gain attention. The animals were duly recovered, but the ewe died in days. As can be imagined, Cheney was not Pinnock's greatest admirer. Being disabled, Pinnock had a problem with his right leg and walked with use of a stick, tending to drag his right leg and foot as he walked. It was possibly this disability that made him such an awkward individual. He wanted and needed to be noticed for something other than his disability, which was a source of low self-esteem for him.

At 12.45 p.m. on Thursday, 6 July 1855, Sarah Driver and her mother, Rhoda Tye, were quietly walking along the public footpath from Kettering towards Rothwell. It was a pleasant day and the pair had been enjoying a stroll in the sun; neither of them could have envisaged what they were about to encounter. As they turned a corner and approached a stile in the footpath they saw a blood-covered human body lying across their route. As they got closer to the form, they recognised it as Benjamin Cheney, an 81-year-old farmer from Rothwell. He lay on his back and was clearly dead. It was carnage; there was blood everywhere, and Ben had been the victim of a nasty attack. As they looked round they saw that the unfortunate man's brains lay strewn across the footpath and along the grass verge. The women felt sick and at once made their way to Rothwell and summoned the police, who went directly to the scene. On arrival, the officers noted a single and particularly nasty-looking wound behind the dead man's left ear. The wound measured four inches long and was two inches deep, going deep into the cranium and releasing brain tissue.

It wasn't too long before the police had a suspect. Further inquiries revealed that Isaac Pinnock had been seen hanging around the stile a few minutes before the women had made the shocking discovery. In fact, Samuel Taylor could confirm that he had seen Pinnock rushing, as best he could, along the footpath at around 12.42 p.m.

As if this wasn't sufficient evidence in itself to put a suspect at the scene of the crime, a set of footprints could be clearly seen leading from the crime scene back towards Rothwell. These were made by someone who walked with the aid of a walking stick. The footprint for the left foot was perfect. However, the suspect obviously had a deformity of some kind to his right foot or leg, as there was a scrape or drag-mark where this had been put down. The footprints were followed to a point where they became indistinct, and there, lying in the long grass, a blood-covered axe with human brain tissue and hair on its blade was found. This was evidently the murder weapon. It was later confirmed that the axe belonged to the father of Isaac Pinnock.

Pinnock was duly arrested and charged with murder and robbery after he confessed to killing the old man and stealing 14 shillings and 6 pence from his pockets. He was found guilty of murder and robbery, and sentenced to hang. Later this sentence was minimised, mainly through his disability and by virtue of the fact that his intention was not to murder but to commit robbery. The death-penalty sentence was commuted to life imprisonment.

The crimes of James Shaw, a 25-year-old who hailed from Banbury, were equally as grotesque. He was, without doubt, the most despicable sort of criminal and killer one could imagine. His crimes were so atrocious as to still arouse great emotion, over a century after they occurred. On the morning of Saturday, 10 July 1897, James Shaw visited the home of his brother-in-law, Frank Smith, in Stuchbury. Finding only his niece Alice, aged nine, and nephew Albert, aged thirteen, at home, he elected to take the children out for a walk in the countryside. They went happily with their Uncle Jim. After a short distance, out in the fields, Shaw took advantage of his position and sexually abused young Alice before sending her home in a terrible state. His nephew Albert, who was the only witness to the sexual act, remained with Shaw and was never again seen alive.

When Albert had failed to return home the following day, the police were alerted. The circumstances surrounding the investigation that followed allowed the investigating officers to plot James Shaw's precise movements, and those of the two children as well. Emma Smith, Alice and Albert's older sister, had seen the three of them walking through the village at around 2 p.m. Joseph Franklin, meanwhile, could place them in the field at Stone Pits shortly after 2 p.m. Walter Kent confirmed that he saw James Shaw walking away from Stuchbury at around 4.00 p.m. and it was around the same time that Alice was seen returning home by Martha Wootton. A publican recalled serving Shaw with a beer later in the afternoon and described his appearance as 'wild and strange-looking'.

A search party was hurriedly formed and an officer was sent to speak with James Shaw to ask where he had left and last seen the children. He claimed that he said goodbye to them both at the village blacksmith's in Stuchbury. Buildings, outhouses and barns were searched, as was local woodland, but yielded nothing. Police Constable Coles was the unlucky person who found the remains of young Albert. He first came across the torso, minus its head. The wound around the neck region was jagged and torn: there was no doubting the fact that the boy's head had been crudely chopped from his body and then tossed away. It was found shortly after, twenty feet away from the torso in some long grass. A bloodstained open-bladed razor was also found, lying close to the body and, judging by the congealed blood and flesh that stuck to its blade, was clearly the instrument used to remove the boy's head. Without any delay, James Shaw was arrested and remanded in custody. In prison, he became violent, attacking prison guards and fellow inmates. He tried to commit violent suicide on a number of occasions and had to be restrained from doing so by several guards. In court, because of these violent outbursts and his agitated state, he was flanked by a number of formal officers who would restrain him if necessary. A plea of insanity was given but dismissed, and the jury found him guilty of murder and he was sentenced to death. Later, however, he was re-examined by doctors, who declared him insane, and therefore his penalty was commuted to detention in a criminal lunatic asylum for life. Hardly a punishment to fit the crime!

Chapter 2

Witches Galore
1600s

*Did witchcraft truly abound in the quiet rural areas
of Northampton? Find out why the Witchfinder General
himself visited Northampton.*

Nothing strikes fear into the soul quite like the mention of witchcraft. It's something of a taboo subject that, when raised in conversation, causes either alarm and distress or utter contempt, as people would prefer to remain deliberately ignorant of its purpose and methods. I am certain that it won't come as any surprise to you to learn that witchcraft is still practised around the world, but it's not all a case of black magic rituals or highly motivated and sexually explicit cults dancing naked round an open fire. Such descriptive narratives may well be ideal subject matter for the gutter press, such as the case reported in a Sunday national that caused such a sensation in and around east Northamptonshire in the not too distant past, for example. It was alleged in the article that people of some standing in the public eye were actually practising witches, and were found naked and acting very peculiarly in some woods. To be honest, the whole incident sounded extremely sordid and was possibly a cause of great embarrassment to those concerned! It's

*Matthew Hopkins, the famous
Witchfinder of Manningtree.*

The witches' dance, led by Satan.

probably best to leave that tale where it belongs: in the county's dark and often secretive woodland areas.

Over the years, Northamptonshire has had a strong association with witchcraft of all types; in fact it was part of the East Anglia group that gained some notoriety in the seventeenth and eighteenth centuries for the amount of witchcraft purported to be taking place within the county boundaries.

Witchcraft first really came to light in Britain in 1468 when the German-born Dominican inquisitors Jacob Sprenger and Heinrich Kramer penned the definitive witchcraft volume that was intended to help suppress witchcraft worldwide, *Malleus Maleficarum* (The Hammer of Witchcraft). The book fundamentally set goals for identifying witches and methods for their persecution. The publication was actually followed by a slump in witch-hunting, but by the start of the seventeenth century, in Britain anyway, it was on the increase, and the poor folk who were identified through 'tried and tested' means as

Torture for those found guilty of witchcraft.

practising witches often met the most gruesome end.

Agnes Brown and Joan Vaughan were a mother and daughter from Guilsborough. Joan, it was alleged at her trial at the Assizes in Northampton castle, had offended Elizabeth Belcher, wife of the Lord of the manor of Guilsborough, Dadbridgecourt Belcher. Elizabeth had retaliated and apparently struck Joan with no great force, but the woman was immediately seized with violent pain. Believing that she was bewitched, she therefore accused Joan and her mother of being witches.

There is an ancient superstition that, to purge a witch's curse, the witch herself must be scratched so as to draw blood. So with this purpose in mind, Elizabeth's brother visited the house of the two women with the sole intention of scratching them. As he approached the house he was 'suddenly stopped and could not enter'. 'Twice or thrice he tried to go to the house, he was still stayed.' A short time afterwards, the brother suffered exactly the same pains as his sister; in consequence of this, he too made accusations of witchcraft against Joan Vaughan and her mother.

The two women were arrested and taken to Northampton jail. While there, they were visited by Elizabeth Belcher and her brother, who still held aspirations to scratch them.

This they did, and it is said that they were 'suddenly delivered of their pain Howbeite they fell again into their old trances and were more violently tormented then ever.'

Returning home from Northampton in a horse-drawn coach, the brother and sister apparently noticed strange apparitions of a man and woman on horseback. Noting many strange gestures from the spectres, the brother shouted out that either they or their horses should miscarry. Immediately the horses fell down dead. In light of this most spurious evidence, Joan Vaughan and Agnes Brown were found guilty of witchcraft.

In another part of the county, Arthur Bill, of Raunds, was also accused of being a 'witch'. He and his parents were accused inasmuch as they allegedly bewitched to death a woman and some of her cattle. The poor Bill family were put to the test by a cruel and frightful method, 'Ordeal by Water'. This grotesque act had the victims secured, their thumbs being tied to their big toes, and they would then be thrown into a pond. To float would show they were guilty of being a witch, to sink would mean innocence, but sinking would clearly also mean death by drowning. All of the Bill family floated.

Arthur Bill was incarcerated in Northampton jail to await execution; his father, for unknown reasons, was neither jailed nor hanged, and nothing more is known of him. Arthur Bill's mother cheated the hangman by slitting her own throat and bleeding to death.

Meanwhile, Helen Jenkinson, of Thrapston, was accused of bewitching a child to death and of manifesting images of toads and snakes on the linen of the midwife who searched her. Mary Barber, of Stanwick, was accused of bewitching a man to death. All three individuals were accused and found guilty of witchcraft, and hanged on the permanent gallows in Abington village on Sunday, 22 July 1612. There were countless others too who died as a result of the witchcraft persecutions. For instance, it is recorded that a 'young man of Denford' was hanged for sending an imp to stampede a man's cattle.

By 1645, the Witchfinder General, Matthew Hopkins, and his assistant, John Stearne, were cleansing the East Anglia region of witches, distributing their own unique form of practice for identifying a witch and providing confirmed evidence for the subsequent trial. Few escaped the clutches of this group once they had come to their attention, and those who didn't confess would suffer greatly. Hopkins's team, which consisted of Stearne and Mary Philips, would often starve suspects of sleep and food. They were then walked up and down a small room until they were fit to drop, and finally they would submit and confess to whatever they were told.

In 1646, Stearne, it is recorded, was active in east Northamptonshire seeking out witches. At Denford, a farmer by the name of Cox accused a young man in the parish of being a witch after he had asked for a job on his farm, and was told there was none. The cattle ran so violently away, foaming at the mouth to such effect that the farmer had to get on his horse to round them up. The young man confessed, after a gruelling interrogation by Stearne, to sending an imp to torment the cattle.

Elsewhere, in 1646, Anne Goodfellow, of Woodford, stated that the Devil appeared to her in the form of a white cat, shortly after the death of her aunt. The devil spoke to her in a low voice and told her not to

Witchfinder General Matthew Hopkins confronting two witches and their 'imps'.

be afraid as he was her aunt's spirit. He asked her to deny God, Christ and her Baptism, which she said she did. He promised her that she would be saved and that he would do for her what she desired. He then asked for her blood to seal the covenant, and bit her second finger, drawing blood, which he took in his mouth. She called the Devil a filthy liar, as she was as poor as ever after this!

In Rushden, widow Elizabeth Currey was interrogated by Stearne. The poor woman actually confessed that some years earlier she had made love to the Devil, and so denied God, through her wilfulness, and poverty, with a desire for revenge. At Burton Latimer, meanwhile, Stearne made female witches confess to being transported through the air to their local gatherings.

A most curious event, which clearly depicts how witchcraft was suspected and alleged, took place in Thrapston in 1646. It involved Assistant Witchfinder John Stearne and a 'very aged man' from Thrapston called Cherry.

The basis of the allegations arises from the situation of Sir John Washington, who was Lord of the manor. The family lived in Thrapston, though their ancestral home was at Sulgrave Manor. Washington had initially married in 1621 and fathered four boys with his wife, before she died in 1624. Remarrying, he had a daughter and a further son. By 1639 both children from the second marriage were dead, and to add to his misery, by the start of the civil war, three of the sons from his first marriage had also died. A sad and bitter man, by 1646 he became overwhelmed by his anguish and grew suspicious of everything. Washington noticed that now his cattle began to die, and wondered why; it was then that he heard local gossip about an incident relating to an old man he knew too well – old man Cherry.

Seemingly, a local farmer had died of a diseased tongue, which by the time he died had hung from his mouth by its roots. Before losing his speech he had told of how he had crossed words with an old man called Cherry over his dog, which had scared the farmer's cattle. During the exchange, Cherry had apparently wished that the farmer's tongue would rot from his head, which of course it had! Washington heard of this and, as soon as John Stearne arrived in town, had the witchfinder notified of the suspicious deaths surrounding his family members, and now of his cattle and how he now believed Cherry was responsible.

Stearne soon confronted the old man and commenced intense interrogation of the suspected witch. Cherry had little in the way of options left to him, and being old, he was easy to break down into a confessional state. As a result he admitted to making a pact with the

A
CONFIRMATION
And Difcovery of
WITCH CRAFT,

Containing thefe feverall particulars ;

That there are VVitches called
bad Witches, and Witches untruely called
good or white Witches , and what manner of
people they be , and how they may bee knowne ;
with many particulars thereunto tending.

Together with the Confeffions of many of thofe executed fince
May 1645. in the feverall Counties hereafter mentioned.
As alfo fome objections Anfwered.

By *John Stearne,* now of *Lawfhall* neere *Burie*
Saint *Edmonds* in *Suffolke,* fometimes of
Manningtree in *Effex.*

PROV.17.15. *He that juftifieth the wicked, and he that condemneth the juft, even they*
both are an abomination to the Lord.
DEVT. 13.14. *Thou fhalt therefore inquire , and make fearch, and afke diligently,*
whether it be truth, and the thing certaine.

LONDON,
Printed by *William Wilfon,* dwelling in Little Saint *Bartholo-*
mewes neere *Smithfield.* 1 6 4 8. —

John Stearne's book of confessions outlining his activity in Northampton.

Devil, sending imps to kill the farmer with whom he had quarrelled
over his dog, and to at least two more suspicious deaths in the area.
The old man was quickly taken to Northampton jail, where he died
before being tried.

During his incarceration a jailor noticed that Cherry's coat was ripped down the back and that his mouth had been plugged by an object. The blockage was cleared from his throat and mouth and the old man, gasping for breath, said that he had just returned from a bridge in Thrapston. The jailer believed him to be delusional and ignored the statement, until a short time later when Cherry was found dead with a ligature round his neck. Assistant Witchfinder Stearne noted of his death, 'A just judgement of God.'

Thereafter, tales of witchery continued throughout the county long after the death of Matthew Hopkins and the demise of John Stearne and Mary Philips. For example, it is recorded that a John Wynnick admitted that one day, when he lost his purse and seven shillings in a barn in Thrapston, he got into a rage about this loss. Such was level of cursing and swearing that the Devil appeared in the form of a bear of about the same size as a rabbit. The next day Wynnick returned to the barn and found his purse, and the small bear turned into a rat and sealed their pact by drawing some blood from the side of his head.

Another so-called witch to be executed in the county was Ann Foster, an old woman. Her crime was that she had long been observed muttering to herself. Allegations that she was a witch and performed witchcraft were based around the behaviour of horses and cattle and a flock of sheep belonging to Joseph Weedon, a rich farmer of Eastcote (just north of Towcester), and with Satan, her colleague, set his house and barns on fire. Foster was arrested and taken to Northampton jail where,

The keepers caused her to be chained to a post that was in the gaol; but she had not been long so tied before she began to swell in all parts of her body, that her skin was ready to burst, which caused her to cry out in the most lamentable manner, insomuch that they were forced to unchain her again, and to give her more liberty that the devil might come to suck her, the which he usually did, his coming constantly about the dead time of night in the likeness of a rat, which at his coming, made the most lamentable and hideous noise which affrighted the people which did belong to the gaol, which caused many to come and see her during her abode there, and several hath been with her and Devil hath been coming to her, but could see nothing but things like Rats, and heard a most terrible noise.

She was hanged at Northampton on 22 August 1674.

The last two people to be hanged for witchcraft in not only the county, but the country, were Elinor Shaw and Mary Phillips of Oundle. The pair were accused of

> *bewitching and tormenting in a diabolical manner the wife of Robert Wise, of Benefield, till she died, also killing by witchcraft, and wicked fascination, one Elizabeth Gorham of Glapthorne, a child of about four years of age, also for bewitching to death one Charles Ireland of Southwick and also for killing several horses, hogs and sheep being the goods of Matthew Gorham, father of the said child aforesaid.*

The evidence used to determine their guilt was the two women's own confession to witchcraft, which had been obtained by two constables who had simply threatened them with death. The death of Mrs Wise had allegedly been caused by the women roasting a wax effigy of her and sticking it full of pins. Both women were found guilty and sentenced to be 'hanged till they were almost dead, and then surrounded with faggots, pitch and other combustible matter, which being set on fire their bodies are to be consumed to ashes.'

An eye-witness account of their execution taken from the book *Execution in Northampton* states:

> *They were so hardened in their wickedness that they publicly boasted that their master (the Devil) would not suffer them to be executed, but they found him a liar, for on Saturday morning, being the 17th inst., they were carried to the gallows on the north side of the town, whither numerous crowds of people went to see them die, and being come to the place of execution the minister repeated his former pious endeavours, to bring them to sense of their sins, but to as little purpose as before; for instead of calling on God for mercy, nothing was heard of them but damning and cursing; however, a little before they tied up, at the request of the minister, Elinor Shaw confessed not only the crime for which she dyed but openly declared before them all how she first became a witch, as did also Mary Phillips; and being desired to say their prayers, they both set up a very loud laughter, calling for the devil to come and help them in such a blasphemous manner as is not fit to mention; so that the sheriff seeing their presumptuous impenitence, caused them to be executed with all the expedition possible, even while they were cursing*

and raving; and as they lived the devils true factors, so they resolutely dyed in his service to the terror of all the people who were eye witnesses to their dreadful and amazing exits.

It would be all too easy to dismiss witchcraft as ineffective and harmless and, more importantly, a thing of the past. However, I know of at least one twentieth-century murder that took place in rural Warwickshire, which had definite witchcraft connotations, the victim being killed in a ritualistic fashion. There, an entire community (though probably aware of the identity of the killer) remained tight-lipped, and the killer escaped justice, dying of natural causes some years later. One thing is certain: witchcraft will always arouse suspicion among those who know nothing about it. Certainly those in this chapter who delved into it, or even dabbled with its supposed power, gained no profit or satisfaction from it at all.

Chapter 3

Prime Suspects
1802 and 1812

Two prime ministers with a local connection to murder,
one as a victim, one as a relative of a killer!
Who are they?

During the early part of the nineteenth century, murder occurred with such alarming frequency as to become almost an accepted part of life. In rural communities in Northamptonshire, a number of murders resulted from disputes over land, and ownership squabbles between farmers over crop rights or between farm workers over tool rights. These kinds of murder were alarmingly common in all rural areas.

One such case occurred on 26 February 1802. The facts surrounding the case are limited and few. I recount them direct from their newspaper source.

William Roberts charged by the coroner's inquest with feloniously killing and slaying Matthew Teat at Ringstead. A sudden dispute arose between Roberts and the deceased while they were working in the harvest field and which terminated by them striking two or three times at each other with scythes. Teat unfortunately received a deep cut across the inside of his lower leg and bled to death in the space of a few minutes.

Roberts was convicted of manslaughter, fined one shilling and sent to prison for one month. This is believed to be the last recorded dual with scythes to take place in the county.

We can be forgiven for thinking this was a rather lenient sentence for such a dastardly act, although by today's standards this crime was fairly unremarkable, and would hardly merit any attention in a modern book on a subject such as murder. Incredibly, it went virtually

Fields around Ringstead, where William Roberts committed his murder.

unnoticed and unrecorded anywhere for a period of almost two centuries. At face value, then, this crime has little in the way of importance and almost unassumingly avoids notoriety. That is until one delves further.

The said William Roberts was married and had three sons and a daughter from the relationship. His eldest son, John, also married and himself had three sons. It is from these three sons that some notoriety does surface, for it is from these family members that Baroness Margaret Thatcher (one-time British Prime Minister) is descended. Baroness Thatcher was Margaret Roberts before her marriage to the late Dennis Thatcher, and her family moved from Northamptonshire to Grantham, Lincolnshire, just after the turn of the twentieth century. At the time this story was first revealed, Baroness Thatcher, as she is now known, was still in office as Prime Minister, and not unreasonably, her office declined to make any comment on the matter.

Not many people with such a public profile and in a position of high office would wish it known that one of their ancestors had been convicted of manslaughter!

Just ten years after this event, in 1812, another crime with strong Northampton links occurred, again related to a Prime Minister. The assassination of Prime Minister Spencer Perceval in the lobby of the House of Commons in the early evening of Monday, 11 May 1812 caused the entire nation to recoil in horror. The right honourable gentleman, First Lord of the Treasury, was also at the time Member of Parliament for Northampton. He had a home in the town, which he used when on parliamentary business in the county, as well as a marital home close to Ealing Common, in Ealing, West London.

Spencer Perceval.
L. B. Ealing

While making his way through the busy lobby he was shot in the left breast by an assassin, and cried out 'Murder!' or 'Murderer!' as he collapsed to the lobby floor. It took fully twelve minutes for him to die. Meanwhile, his killer was detained at the scene. It should, however, be noted that during the ensuing frenzy, a number of different people were believed to be suspects, including two gentlemen who were sent to fetch a doctor but were deemed by many witnesses to be perpetrators fleeing from the scene! So it was with some concern that those who detained the guilty man, complete with pistol on his person, asked the question of him, 'Are you the killer?' He replied, 'I am that unhappy man.'

The Prime Minister, Spencer Perceval, was in fact murdered by John Bellingham, a 32-year-old mentally disturbed man who originally hailed from St Neots in Huntingdonshire. Bellingham, for a number of months, had been on something of a crusade. He blamed the Prime Minister for what he believed to be a serious miscarriage of justice that he had suffered in Russia, causing him to be incarcerated. In an attempt to get the British government's attention and response over the issue, he had plagued parliament with letters of complaint, seeking some form of financial reimbursement and causing those he believed to have failed him to be investigated and brought to justice. He even wrote to the Bow Street Runners telling them of the ill fate he had endured as a result of the failing of the British government. This similarly elicited no response.

It has to be said that in the main the missives sent to parliament were ignored, but due to their quantity, they were eventually, though cursorily, investigated. The British authorities looked into the case John Bellingham offered and decided that there were no substantive grounds on which he could base his allegations. The clear inference of their findings was that his incarceration was to some extent self-induced.

As a result of the negative outcome of the inquiry, Bellingham became a bitter and twisted man. He placed the blame for his current position as a financially poor man solely at the government's door. Lord Gower,

John Bellingham, killer of Spence Perceval.

he claimed, had failed to help him when he was wrongfully imprisoned in Russia. Gower later (after Bellingham's execution) tried to disprove this claim by writing to the press and stating that he had in fact managed to secure Bellingham's release from incarceration.

Realising his letter-writing was getting him nowhere, Bellingham decided to kill the Prime Minister as retribution. A short time before the murder, he had purchased two pistols and would be seen practise-firing these on Hampstead Heath. He had also taken to frequently visiting the House of Commons and getting to know its internal workings intimately. He would see ministers passing to and fro in some of its great halls. So calm was his state of mind before the incident, it is now known that he was with his landlady from his New Millman Street lodgings, looking at paintings just hours before committing the murder. He had left her, adding as he did so that he had some unattended business to see to. There can be no doubting then, that it was a premeditated and well-executed crime.

At the subsequent trial Bellingham said, 'I have been denied the redress of my grievance by government; I have been ill treated.' In a trial that lasted just eight hours, during which Bellingham defended himself but admitted his guilt, there could be only one outcome. He was found guilty of murder and ultimately hanged outside Newgate prison at 8.00 a.m. on 18 May 1812. During his term of imprisonment before execution, there was a good amount of political and public sympathy, with anti-government graffiti being daubed on specific government buildings in the capital.

Portrait of Spencer Perceval painted from his death mask. L. B. Ealing

No consideration was given to the state of mind of the prisoner although it is clear that he was suffering from some form of mental disability. There was no provision in English law for what we would now call 'diminished responsibility'. This facet of the English legal system did not come into being until 1843. That said, one gets the distinct feeling that Bellingham would have hanged irrespective of whether this judicial option was available or not.

Surely few counties can claim two murderous links to British prime ministers.

Chapter 4

Once, Twice, Three Times Murder
1821

In almost comical proportions, because of love,
a man tries to kill his lover's husband, not once, not twice,
but three times. Finally he achieved his goal, but at what cost?

The village and community of Charwelton lie close to the western border of Northamptonshire, about seven miles from Daventry. Today there is little to remind us of how it used to be; the old village is now known as Church Charwelton. In the sixteenth century a farmhouse was built on the outskirts of the village, along the Priors Marston–Hellidon Road. It was a large property called Cherwell House. In 1821 the house was owned by a wealthy farmer by the name of John Clarke, who was sixty-seven years old. His wife, Mary, was a mere thirty-five and, perhaps understandably, dissatisfied with her position as the wife of a much older man. It wasn't as though Clarke had a great deal to offer his young wife: he had been a farmer and landowner for most of his life and this was where his passion lay. Indeed, there is much to suggest that Mary Clarke was little more than a trophy to the farmer.

Unknown to John Clarke, Mary had been playing the field more than a little, and had conducted a string of illicit relationships behind her husband's back. By 1821, her latest lover was a farm labourer known as Phillip Haynes. It is said that Haynes had in fact been in a sexual relationship with Mary for over seven years and that, prior to her marriage to Clarke, Mary had given birth to a child by Haynes, who had been farmed out to her close friends. Sadly the child died within a year of being born. Soon after this, Mary moved into Cherwell House with Clarke. As his mistress (of sorts), this allowed her some financial gain and reward.

One morning, after a violent quarrel had taken place at the

farmhouse, Mary left Clarke and ran away to Northampton. She could bear no more of his elderly mannerisms and idiosyncrasies. It seems likely that Clarke had found out that Mary was not the young darling he had thought she was, but was abusing his wealth and flirting outrageously with anyone who took her fancy. Despite this, he was not keen to lose her – they had formed a friendship which he enjoyed – so he engaged his friend Edward Turland to try to find Mary and bring her back to the farm. It wasn't long before she was found and Turland told the young woman that Clarke wished to marry her. The thought of being legal beneficiary to Clarke's wealth greatly thrilled her, and without hesitation she accepted the offer to return, and even more enthusiastically, his offer of marriage. After a discussion with Haynes the pair decided that it would be in their long-term interest to go ahead with the marriage. Two children were born of the relationship, though, as one can imagine, the actual identity of the father is open to conjecture. Mary requested that her mother be allowed to move into the farm to help with the upbringing of the children; her husband agreed and very soon the women were controlling almost every piece of business at the farm.

In February 1819, Mary somehow persuaded her husband to employ Phillip Haynes as a general labourer. It wasn't long before Haynes, who was, to be fair, a hard-working man, was openly displaying too much attention to the farmer's wife. Clarke duly sacked Haynes and evicted him from the room he had provided. Surreptitiously, Mary contacted her close friends John and Elizabeth Bush at nearby Byfield and arranged for Haynes to lodge with them until further notice. Elizabeth had been a close personal friend of Mary for a long time and had been present at the birth of each of her 'official' children.

Elizabeth would visit Mary at Cherwell House and pass communications between Haynes and her friend, without John Clarke being aware. As the days turned into weeks the lovers' longings to live together grew stronger. Suddenly the love letters took a different, more sinister turn, as Mary began to contemplate murder. Her husband was too fit and healthy and therefore not expected to die in the foreseeable future. To eliminate him would allow the couple to get together and would also provide wealth beyond their dreams.

Mary asked Phillip Haynes to kill her husband, and so besotted was the man with Mary that he was prepared to commit to this pact. Murder would not, Haynes thought, be difficult to commit; he had seen enough animals slaughtered and killed during his farm work, so someone he regarded as his enemy would not be a difficult proposition. He knew that farm work could be dangerous and so, understanding that any murder would have to look like a farming accident, he began to plan how he would commit the act. This set in motion a series of ridiculous attempts by the illicit lovers to rid themselves of John Clarke.

The first attempt came late one evening when John Clarke was returning home alone after visiting friends in a nearby village. His horse was galloping at high speed, and the animal turned into a small copse close to Cherwell House. Suddenly Clarke felt a stinging pain to his chest and was thrown backwards from the saddle and off the horse. Shaken, he got to his feet and fumbled about in the darkness. He recalled his horse and stared into the gloomy darkness to see what it was that had thrown him from his ride. There before him was a rope which had been attached between two trees close to the entrance of the copse. It was a sturdy rope but was at such a height as to cause no serious harm to Clarke. The person who had put it there had possibly done so out of mischief more than intent to injure. Clarke felt it was possibly the work of a child or local footpads or robbers. Cutting the rope down, he mounted his horse and returned home. The following day he alerted his neighbours to his concerns and warned them of travelling late at night in case of assault and robbery.

Mary Clarke was livid with her lover and told him she was ashamed of his half-hearted attempt at killing her husband. He would have to show much more cunning and guile to kill her husband off. Haynes was motivated by this and told Mary that her husband would soon be dead.

Late one winter evening in 1820, Haynes lay in wait by a gated wall close to the farmhouse. In his hand was a large wooden club he had manufactured for the purpose of murder. It was not long before the unsuspecting Clarke came by the gate and, without warning, he was clubbed to the ground from behind. Stunned, he attempted to snatch a glimpse of his attacker, but his vision was obviously distorted by the light or lack of it, as he later described the attacker as being short and wearing a red striped waistcoat. Haynes was tall and slim and incredibly was not one of Clarke's suspects. Within days of this incident, Haynes purchased some poison (laudanum) and sent it to Mary so that she should try to administer it to her husband in his tea. However, the dose was insufficient and simply made Clarke vomit.

The situation was now verging on the ludicrous, as Mary urged her lover to act with haste and to make a real effort at murder. She took the lead and told Haynes to purchase a pistol and to shoot Clarke; he could then abandon the weapon and flee the scene, and she would discuss with the authorities the previous attempts on Clarke's life and blame robbers who were in the area. Haynes didn't like this plan but was forced to go along with it after his lover threatened him with ending the relationship.

He soon purchased a horse pistol, some gunpowder and large shot, from a shop on Market Hill in Brackley. So, armed with the loaded pistol on the morning of 8 February 1821, Haynes made his way to Cherwell House to finally kill John Clarke.

He climbed into a hen roost in a barn close to the farmhouse. From this position he could get a clear view of everyone who came and went from the farm buildings. He made a small den for himself among the hay and was visited and given food and drink by Mary Clarke. Haynes became very nervous at the enormity of the task that lay ahead of him, and couldn't bring himself to pull the trigger and so commit murder. Mary would have none of it and continued to harass Haynes, calling him cowardly and weak. So, on Saturday, 10 February at around four o'clock in the afternoon Phillip Haynes fired the shot which was to kill John Clarke. The shot hit the farmer on the elbow and on the upper left arm. The initial wound was so large that the doctor who attended the injured man could easily insert two fingers into the entry point of the wound and feel the splintered bone beneath.

Clarke was forced to retire to his bed. The surgeon who attended from Badby examined him and advised him that the arm would have to be amputated before gangrene set in. The farmer, realising that his life was ebbing away, insisted on making a will so that his affairs could be settled on his death. The surgeon delayed the operation until this was done. Eventually, the limb was successfully removed, and when it

A Copy of Verses,

ON THE UNFORTUNATE MAN AND WOMAN

Phillip Haynes,

AND

Mary Clarke,

Who was Executed at Northampton March 10, 1821

FOR THE

Wilful Murder of John Clarke,

Husband to the latter at the parish of Charwelton, Northamptonshire.

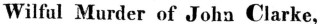

Good people all of each degree,
Give ear unto my tragedy,
Which I am going to unfold,
It is as true as e'er was told.

At Charwelton Northamptonshire,
A wealthy farmer lived there,
One Mr. Clarke he had a wife,
But lived a most unhappy life.

His wicked wife we understand,
Connected got with her servant man,
One Phillip Haynes that was his name
From Adstone, Northamptonshire, he came.

Their intimacy it got so,
That all her secrets let him know,
Persuading him day after day,
To take her husbands life away.

Then this unfortunate Phillip Haynes,
For carnal lust and cursed gains.
Soon yielded to her cruel will,
Her husband Mr. Clarke to kill.

Then unto Brackley he did steer,
Into a shop he entered there,
He bought a gun, powder and shot,
To execute the cruel plot.

To Mary Clarke he did return,
Who's heart with cruelty did burn,
And told her he had obeyed her rules,
For he had got the fatal tools.

To scheming then they did proceed,
The safest place to do the deed,
Says Haynes I'll go into the barn,
For there no one can me discern.

Or where I am no one can tell,
Says Mary Clarke that's very well,
For there in secret you can stay,
Amongst the barley night and day.

Until that you have done the deed,
I'll bring you every thing you need,

So back and forward Haynes did go,
Unto the barn as you shall know.

From February the 8th day,
Until the 10th Haynes there did stay,
When Mr Clarke without regard,
Then came into the hay rick yard.

Then straight upon the rick he got,
When from the barn Haynes at him shot,
Which gave to Clarke his mortal wound,
And brought him soon unto the ground

And as upon the ground he lay,
I'm done, I'm done, Clarke he did say,
When cruel Haynes heard him say so
He knew he'd gave the fatal blow.

Then this vile murderer he did creep,
Into the barley mow so deep,
Thinking to get out of the snare,
But soon he was discovered there.

Then he confessed the cruel deed.
And to Northampton sent with speed,
So now we'll leave him there to mourn
And unto Mary Clarke return.

Who in short time she taken were,
And lodg'd with Haynes to take a share
For their sad act of cruelty,
while blood for vengeance loud doth cry

At the assizes they were brought,
To answer for their cruel fault,
The Jury soon did guilty cry,
And they were both condemned to die.

And on the 10th of March they were,
Brought up the awful fate to share,
That day upon the gallows tree,
They suffered for their cruelty,

Now let their fate a warning be,
To all of high and low degree,
Be constant to your bosom friend,
Then God will bless you to the end.

T. Bloomer, Printer, 42, Edgbaston Street, Birmingham,

Reprinted for Northamptonshire Libraries, 1976, at the Alden Press, Oxford

Reprinted verses on Phillip Haynes and Mary Clarke.

was examined, traces of lead shot were found in the splintered bone.

In the meantime, the person who fired the shot was still at large on the farm. A cursory search of farm buildings revealed nothing, but high in the hen roost, hidden among the hay in the barn was Phillip Haynes, watching everything taking place below him. He was forced to remain in hiding there until the commotion surrounding the shooting had calmed down. He would have been safe but for the keen perception of farm labourer Anthony Marriott. Marriott had been standing in front of Clarke when he was shot, and saw a puff of gunsmoke emerging from the barn moments after his master fell to the floor. In the confusion, Marriott had forgotten about this, and he knew the outbuildings of the farm had already been searched, so it was unlikely that he would resolve anything by carrying out another search of the barn. However, the gunsmoke continued to bother Marriott, so he decided to take a look in the barn on Monday, 12 February. He focussed his attention on the hayloft and walked around it, tentatively prodding at the hay with a pitchfork. Suddenly he felt the fork make contact with something beneath the hay and, stopping, he turned round and again prodded into the same spot, this time with some force. Without warning Haynes emerged from the hay and yelled out, 'Be civil and I will stand up!' Marriott was angered and shouted back at the man, whom he recognised, 'You rascal, I have a good mind to stab you – you did not mind killing my master!' As inaccurate as this statement was at the time, it is clear that the wound had been accepted as being fatal.

Haynes was led from the barn and handed over to the authorities. News of the apprehending spread to John Clarke, who was now on his deathbed, and asked for the prisoner to be brought to his bedside at once. Haynes was taken into the bedroom, where the wounded man pointed to him and said, 'You bloody-minded fellow, how could you do me such an unkind act?' Haynes denied the shooting and pleaded for Clarke's mercy. The dying farmer would have none of it and told the authorities to take him away without delay. John Clarke passed away at four o'clock the following morning.

A search of the prisoner was carried out, and inside his coat pocket was found a quantity of lead shot and, more incriminating, a love letter from Mary Clarke. Further letters were found when Haynes's lodgings at Byfield were searched. These contained all the details of different attempts on John Clarke's life and, of course, the planning for the shooting which was to lead to murder. Haynes continued to deny his involvement and said that he had been framed. Mary Clarke, meanwhile, remained at liberty for a further week, before she too was arrested for murder.

The pair were brought to trial at Northampton assizes and found guilty of murder. Prior to their execution on Northampton Heath, both confessed to the murder and repented their sins. Mary Clarke was visited in the condemned cell by her two children and it is said that the sight of them made her guilt-ridden, hence her confession on the gallows. A large crowd witnessed the execution and both prisoners were clearly agitated at the thought of the fate that awaited them.

Chapter 5

Lydia, Oh Lydia, Where art thou, Lydia? 1850

What happened to Lydia Atley? Was she murdered?
Did they ever find her remains?
A new look at this enduring mystery.

Ringstead is situated in east Northamptonshire between the towns of Raunds and Thrapston. Today it is bypassed by the A605 road and is not readily accessible unless one knows how to find it. It now has a population of more than three thousand. However, back in the mid-nineteenth century, where our interest lies, only a hundred or so folk lived there. In 1850 it was a small but very exposed and vulnerable community, where everyone tended to know everyone else's business, and gossip was rife and, far too often, malicious. Ringstead was, in the main, no different to any other hamlet the length and breadth of the country: busy and reliant on the land as a valuable resource. There was little in the way of social activity, so those with overactive imaginations made their own entertainment. Most folk worked for the gentry, landowners and the like, who in turn looked after their workforce and, in some cases, housed staff. However, this could cause jealousy and ill feeling in some quarters.

Miss Lydia Atley was not the sort of young woman who found herself at the centre of village gossip, good or bad. Somewhat unattractive, she hadn't many male admirers and was a solitary individual. Lydia had suffered much ill fate for someone of her relatively young age. Both her parents had died, leaving her penniless and without any means of income. Being a sincere and polite person, she soon found herself work by taking on cleaning chores in many of the larger houses and properties in the area.

You can imagine, then, the villagers' surprise when Lydia

announced to a friend in July 1850 that she was with child and that the father was a local man. Wherever she went, village folk would ask how she was keeping and suddenly engage her in conversation in an attempt to extricate information or clues about the identity of the father of the child. Cruelly, some people talked of it being by virtue of an encounter with a frequently passing vagrant with whom she had been seen talking on several occasions. Others felt she was lying to attract attention to herself. After all, according to some, she had never been the sort of girl who could attract the attention of men.

Eventually, with so many of the locals prying and second-guessing, she revealed that the father was a local butcher, William Weekley Ball. The gossip was now in full swing and rather barbed. William Ball was already married and, according to all who knew him, happily so. The butcher vehemently denied the association, often quoting his unequivocal love for his wife as evidence against the accusations. Poor Lydia was lambasted by many for spouting such crude untruths and for attempting to damage the marital bliss of the Ball family.

The cruel reality of all this was that Ball was in fact the liar, and not Lydia. A relationship between the couple seemed more than likely. For one thing, many local people could recall seeing the couple walking together through the local countryside. According to Lydia, William Ball had told her that he was intending to leave his wife permanently, and that he wanted to marry her (Lydia). The young woman had believed everything he said and continued with the sexual relationship. However, when she announced that she was pregnant, it all changed. Suddenly William Ball did not want to associate with her. He refused her advances and to engage in any kind of conversation with her.

Lydia visited a close friend, Mrs Groome, on 20 July 1850, she told the woman, whom she trusted and confided in, that she desperately needed some money, and that she intended to get this from William Ball. The reason for her requiring this money is unclear, but it would appear to have been for an abortion, though Lydia did not state this. She did state, however, that she wished she had never met or fallen for the improprieties of William Ball. Mrs Groome was to later recall how agitated, nervous and completely disillusioned Lydia was during this visit, when she realised how she had been duped by Ball with his false promises of marriage. This was the last time Mrs Groome was to sit and talk with her friend.

The evening of 22 July 1850 was a warm and sultry one across Northamptonshire. Local farmer John Hill was out working close to the property owned by William Ball. He noticed the butcher strolling with Lydia Atley in the orchard area of his garden. From what he could see and hear the couple were clearly in dispute. Inquisitively he kept watch and strained his ear to listen to what was being said; could it after all be true that William Ball had made Lydia pregnant? It would be a grand tale to tell if he could witness them in the act of a loving embrace. Suddenly, the farm worker heard Lydia cry out, 'I won't, I won't! It's yours and no one else's!' Then silence. Unable to see what was taking place in the orchard, Hill decided he was wasting his time and so moved off.

Minutes later, Joseph Groome, the husband of Lydia's closest friend, walked past the end of the orchard garden. There was no one else about and he was surprised to suddenly hear voices coming from behind a hedge that surrounded the orchard area. Stopping and getting as close to the hedge as he could so as to hear who was talking, he quickly recognised the voices of Lydia and William Ball. He distinctly heard Lydia say, 'I believe you mean to kill me, Weekley Ball. Lord have mercy on your soul if I am to die in this condition.' The words caused a chill to run down his spine. Surely Ball wouldn't commit such an atrocious act? He stood rooted to the spot for a few minutes, but heard nothing else that aroused his concerns so, believing it to be nothing more than the desperate plea for attention by a scorned lover to a partner, he too continued on his way. On arriving home, he mentioned it to his wife, but relayed it in such a manner that it could be deemed as nothing more than foolish talk by Lydia.

The village grapevine was active and that very same evening there was talk of how Lydia and Ball had been seen together and how it seemed that, justifiably, there was no smoke without fire. Why was he so keen to talk with her if, as he suggested, she was spreading malicious gossip about him? Surely it would be better to stay well clear and avoid any contact and to rise above suspicion? Suddenly there was a groundswell of opinion in favour of Ball actually being the father. Whatever the situation regarding the father's identity, all the salacious gossip that illicit relationships tend to breed soon paled into insignificance. A far greater, more sombre issue was about to emerge; one which held far more serious implications for all concerned. On the

Back Lane, Ringstead, where Lydia Atley would meet her alleged killer, William Ball.

night of 22 July 1850, Lydia Atley quite literally disappeared from the face of the Earth!

As with so many things, it took some time before anyone realised or became suspicious about her absence from the village. Initially there was a common belief, by virtue of Mrs Groome, no doubt, that William Ball had paid out to Lydia the money to go and have an abortion, or money for her to go and start a new life with the child, well away from Ringstead. The people of Ringstead knew that it wasn't the first time affluence had interfered with everyday life and influenced the outcome, and it certainly wouldn't be the last. William Ball was not fazed by the sudden disappearance of Lydia. Ball welcomed the rumours of her moving away from the area and enthusiastically encouraged them. At every opportunity he would continue to deny being the father of Lydia's child.

It wasn't long before suspicious rumours began to flow not only around Ringstead but throughout all of east Northamptonshire. Travellers and visitors had no recollection of anyone matching Lydia's description being seen on the roads or passing through the district. It seemed highly unlikely that she would suddenly elect to up roots and leave the only area she had known for most of her life. She had no known relatives and was quite insular when it came to relocation or even travelling out of the area. Yet now William Ball was suggesting to local folk that this was what she had done! Suspicion soon fell on the butcher. Within a few days of Lydia's disappearance his highly successful butcher's business was struggling, as local people went elsewhere for their meat provisions and made it quite clear that they now suspected him of causing harm to poor Lydia. Added to this torment, his wife suffered greatly from the village gossip, enduring sly whispers and knowing glances day in, day out. Her relationship with her husband was clearly falling apart, and the further pressure of the loss of income compounded their struggles.

Naturally, with rumours that Lydia had come to harm now rife, it wasn't long before the investigating authorities became involved.

There was a strong belief at the time that Ball had murdered the young woman and buried her remains in a new grave in Meeting Lane cemetery. While sounding sensational, this was in fact quite conceivable. A new grave had been dug at the cemetery a couple of days earlier and this had since been filled in. The local constables from Thrapston looked into the matter and had the grave uncovered, revealing the remains of the genuine corpse, but no sign of Lydia. Despite this, the rumours persisted and became more exaggerated until eventually William Ball was arrested on suspicion of murdering Lydia Atley, and later charged with her murder.

Ball continued to deny any involvement in the woman's disappearance, protesting his innocence of all charges and maintaining that he had not physically harmed her. He was taken before magistrates at Wellingborough, where he claimed that he was the victim of village gossip and mischief. Further, he asked how he could be guilty of murder if no body had ever been found. The magistrate agreed and ordered that he be released from custody with immediate effect, a decision which aroused much negative emotion in Ringstead and the surrounding area.

With his marriage faltering and his business literally ruined, William Ball and his wife left Ringstead and set up home and a new butcher's shop business in Ramsay, Huntingdonshire (now Cambridgeshire). There, his business prospered and his contentment gradually returned.

Meanwhile, back in Northamptonshire, life was not so settled. The people of Ringstead knew that Lydia's sudden disappearance was suspicious; they believed she had met an untimely end and they were not about to let the matter drop. Everyone travelling from the area to neighbouring towns and villages or counties would ask if a woman matching Lydia's description had been encountered or had settled in their community. Letters were mailed out in a similar vein, as each and every response was negative. No one, it seems, had seen Lydia Atley after the evening of 22 July 1850. More baffling was the question, if she had been murdered, where were her remains?

Gradually, the enthusiasm to bring Ball to justice waned; there simply was no corroborative evidence to support the claims of murder. Several schools of thought were developed about what happened to Lydia, all of which saw her meeting a rather grisly end. Many believed that with Ball being a butcher, he killed her then chopped her up into small pieces, selling them as meat in his shop, while others believed he had buried her in his orchard garden. The tales merely added further confusion to the case.

A breakthrough occurred on 13 February 1864, fourteen years after her disappearance, when a group of local labourers, who were tasked with clearing ditches around the Ringstead area, were in Keystone Lane. Digging away in the trench running alongside the road they uncovered what appeared to be skeletal remains.

The police and a doctor were called. The remains were confirmed as being human, and a doctor stated that they looked as though they were those of a young woman. One of the labourers confirmed that the remains were those of Lydia Atley; he recognised that in the lower jaw of the skull a tooth was absent. He had pulled this very same tooth from the mouth of Lydia while she alive.

Police were dispatched to Ramsay and William Ball was arrested, brought back to Thrapston, where he was charged with murder. After a two-day hearing before Thrapston magistrates, he was committed for trial at Northampton's March assizes, commencing 25 February 1864. The evidence on which the prosecution would base its case was almost entirely circumstantial, although there were witnesses who could discuss what they heard on the night of 22 July 1850, some fourteen years earlier.

Before the trial could commence, the prosecution case collapsed in its entirety. The same group of labourers who had found the skeletal remains found another skeleton close to the scene of the first discovery.

On this stretch of road the remains were found in 1864.

These were confirmed as being male. Then on 7 March two more skeletons were uncovered; it was seemingly a mass grave.

The new mystery caused a sensation locally. However, before long it was recalled that there had been a gypsy encampment in that area several years earlier. It was further recalled that they had buried some of their dead around the campsite.

William Ball was released from custody and all charges against him dropped. He returned to Ramsay, but soon realised that he was again the subject of suspicion among the local people, who believed him to be a murderer. In a desperate attempt to prove his innocence he returned to Ringstead with his family. Life there was never pleasant for him, and the rumours about him killing Lydia Atley continued long after his death.

On 25 July 1906, a farmer by the name of Tilly revealed that one of his labourers, a Mr Mayes, had been digging out gravel from some of his fields that ran alongside the Thrapston Road. During this operation Mayes had uncovered something hard about eight inches below the surface of the soil. Clearing the mud and gravel from the object, which had the appearance of a large off-white-coloured rock, he rolled it back with the edge of his spade, and then realised it was a

Ringstead Parish Church, where the 1906 remains were buried.

human skull. He ran to fetch Mr Tilly, and both men cleared away the area, revealing a human skeleton. Close by they found what appeared to be a blade and part of a handle from an old-style razor.

The village constable, Mr Sullivan, was fetched, and with him came a crowd of onlookers. Almost immediately stories of William Ball and Lydia Atley circulated. Soon Dr Buckley from Thrapston arrived at the scene. Carrying out a formal examination of the remains he stated that they were those of a female aged between twenty-six and thirty years at the time of her death. A full report was sent to the coroner, Mr Parker, who without further ado declined to instruct an inquiry into the find due to the probability that the skeleton could not be formally identified. With the finding of a blade close by, it would seem a probable perception that the victim had died as a result of a deliberate haemorrhage.

We can never truly know if the remains were those of Lydia Atley. However, we may suppose that they were. There was no other justifiable reason forthcoming for a body to be buried in that location or area. If the remains were thought to be those of a suicide we can confirm that there were no other missing persons in that area during the era in question. Furthermore, if Lydia had committed suicide, why do it there, and how could she bury herself? It is likely that Ball walked Lydia to this spot, slit her throat then buried her on the night of 22 July 1850. The mystery, it saddens me to say, continues.

For many years after the crime, a ballad entitled, 'The Cruel Butcher of Ringstead' was sung. It began;

Come listen to me and a story I'll tell concerning of Lydia Atley.
Who in Ringstead should be
O cruel butcher, he hung should be
For the killing of Lydia Atley.

Chapter 6

The Death of Amelia Litchfield 1880

The combination of a flirtatious wife,
a jealous husband and alcohol results in murder
and a very sad story indeed.

In early August 1880 an incident occurred in the county town of Northampton that aroused much public sympathy, and in other areas, public outrage at the outcome. It all started at the inquest into the death of Mrs Amelia Litchfield, which took place at Northampton Infirmary on Thursday, 5 August 1880.

David Adams was one of the witnesses called before the Coroner, Mr C. C. Becke:

I am a shoe finisher. The deceased was my sister. She was 29, married to George Litchfield. He is a blocker. On Tuesday morning, I met George in Bearward Street and he asked me if I would go for a walk with him to try and find Amelia. She had been away from home all night. We went about, and then after my wife and I left him, we saw my sister Amelia in company with a man named Smith. My wife went into the Rose and Punchbowl *with Mrs Litchfield, to have a glass of beer, and I went to get George. We joined them, and George said to Amelia, 'Let's be friendly and make it up.' She said, 'No, I shan't.' I called for two more glasses of beer but I was refused. I don't think we were drunk, but we were not sober. We had all had a glass or two. We went to the* Black Lion. *He asked her again to be friends, and she said, 'I shan't.' Now we were all the worse for drink, and went to my house, close on five o'clock. George asked his wife to go home with him, and she said she should not.*
Litchfield left us, and about eight o'clock, we went to their house in St

Edmund's Road. Smith was with us. Amelia asked George if he would have some fried fish, but he wouldn't. They were chatting, but I could see they weren't quarrelling. When my wife and I left, Smith also left. The Litchfields were at the door.

At this point there was much discussion as to the precise situation between George and his wife and why there was talk of making it up.

Adams continued, 'I hadn't seen them quarrelling, but she hadn't been home all night and my brother-in-law was trying to be friendly.' The same juror then asked where she had been all night, and Adams was at a loss to explain or answer this question. After further discussion and a question about what happened to Smith after they had left the Litchfields at their home, Adams responded that they had left him at the corner of the street. Adams was then stood down from giving evidence.

Next to take the witness stand was Anne Litchfield.

I am the wife of Thomas Litchfield, publican of the King of Denmark. *George is my brother-in-law, and he lives in the adjoining house. He came in to see me twice, and then went out with his brother-in-law. I saw him come home in the evening. He beckoned his little child, Florence, and said, 'Your mother is down at her brother's. You go to her, and stay until she comes home.' He then told me he was going to bed. Later his wife came along our passage with her brother and asked me if I had seen George. I said 'He's gone to bed.' She said 'He hasn't.' I went upstairs and saw him lying across the bed with his boots on. She was the worse for drink. They all were.*

The Coroner asked Anne if she was sober.

Oh yes, sir. I had never been out. I had got my business to look after. Adams and his wife, and Smith, left the house together, and I heard nothing more until Mrs Bates came in. She said 'Oh, Mrs Litchfield, George has cut his wife's throat.' Before I could get round the counter, Amelia Litchfield herself came up to the door with her throat cut. There were two men in the bar, and I said for God's sake, someone go to the Infirmary with her. She said my name but never spoke again. The two men took her. I did not see George after that. I daren't go into their house by myself, but I sent for a policeman. I afterwards fainted away and I don't remember any more.

A neighbour, Frances Bates, was then called to give evidence.

> *I live opposite the deceased. While I was standing at my window, I saw Adams and his wife leave George and Amelia standing at the door. She snatched away from him, and said 'I shan't. You go in. Go to bed.' She went towards the centre of the railings in front of the house. George followed her, and caught hold of her, trying to pull her away. No blows were struck, but I heard a noise as if he was trying to strangle her. He was leaning over her. I went out to them, and she ran towards me. I could then see that her throat was cut. Litchfield had gone into the house. I ran across to the public house to tell what I had seen, and she came in.*

Police Constable George Berry of Northampton Borough police told the court:

> *On Tuesday evening, I was at home preparing to go out for night duty, when someone came to the door and said I was wanted up the street. I went to Litchfield's house, but I didn't see his wife. I found him in the living room, lying on the floor, face down. I lifted him up and I could see that his throat was cut. A razor lay open on the table. He wanted to go the closet, but I said; 'We must get you to the infirmary.' As we were going along I said 'Whatever made you do this?' He replied 'It's all jealousy. She has not been behaving as she ought to have done towards me.' He asked where his wife was, and I told him I thought she was at the Infirmary. He said 'I hope she's not dead.'*

Mr A. H. Jones, House Surgeon at Northampton Infirmary, was called next.

> *The deceased was brought in at half past nine. I met her at the door and examined the wound. Her throat had been cut from ear to ear. The bleeding had almost stopped, apparently from loss of blood. She was pulse-less, and what little haemorrhage there was came from little veins in the neck. These had been severed, but not great vessels. I stopped the bleeding. The cut was above the windpipe, across and extended into the gullet, almost to the spine. She died about twenty minutes after admission. Before she died, I saw George Litchfield. His throat was also cut, but the injury was superficial. No vessels of any*

consequence were cut. While I attended him, he said 'If only she had acted fair to me, I shouldn't have done it.' Next morning when he was told of the death of his wife, he said 'I didn't mean to kill her.' He is in my charge still, but in custody. He will not be able to appear for some time.

With such overwhelming evidence provided to them the jury had little choice but to respond with a verdict of wilful murder against George Litchfield.

The matter progressed to formal criminal proceedings and a trial. This took place during the Winter Assizes on 27 October 1880, before Lord Justice Baggalley. Acting for the defence was the respected and somewhat theatrical Montagu Williams QC, who prior to this case had defended the notorious murderer Charles Peace at the Central Criminal Court, London, on a charge of murder of a police officer. His defence of Peace focussed on the fact that Peace had not meant to kill the officer but merely to frighten him! At the end of that particular trial, Peace was found guilty. The experience of the Peace trial apparently provided the advocate with a wealth of experience and a more direct manner in which to strike home his point to the jury.

In Northampton, Williams was at his melodramatic best. The final few words of his closing speech were sufficient to bring the sternest juror to their knees and were clearly intended to play on their emotions:

I seek not to steal your minds away, but I do ask you as fathers and as husbands to put a merciful construction on the acts of this man when you are judging of what the quality of the crime is he is guilty of, if he be guilty of crime at all. I don't know that I can do better to pray that the all seeing Providence from whom no secrets are hid, may guide your mind to a true and righteous judgement.

It was, of course, ridiculous for the advocate to infer that George Litchfield may in fact not be guilty of a crime at all. He had slit his wife's throat, ending her life as a result of his own jealousy. The jury left the court and deliberated. On returning to the court they revealed that they had found George Litchfield guilty of manslaughter but not guilty of murder! There was much rejoicing in court among those who supported the shoe worker.

It would seem that the presiding judge, Lord Justice Baggalley, was somewhat surprised by the verdict: he deferred sentencing until the following day, as he required to investigate the sentencing tariffs before imposing punishment on Litchfield.

The following day in court was not the sombre affair one would ordinarily associate with the closing day of what had been a murder trial. The judge, trying to maintain some sense of the jury's verdict, summed up:

> *The jury have taken a merciful view of your case and it is now my duty to pass a sentence consistent with the nature of the offence of which you have been found guilty. That you inflicted the wounds which caused your wife's death, and that you intended to kill her cannot be doubted by anyone. If after brooding over the course of events you possessed yourself of a razor for the purpose of killing her, there would have been no reason to reduce the offence below that of murder. But it has been suggested that your wife's conduct led you to contemplate suicide, and it is further suggested that you got the razor for that purpose, but when your wife declined to go with you into the house, you, under a sudden impulse, attacked her and fatally wounded her. Which of those views is correct, you alone know. The jury gave you the benefit of the doubt. In giving effect to their verdict, I cannot forget the great sanctity that attaches to human life, and I cannot do otherwise than pass on you a sentence of Penal Servitude for the term of five years.*

Several years after the trial, Montagu Williams was to recall how he found himself hounded by supporters of Litchfield who wished to shake him by the hand for his successful defence work: misguided loyalty, indeed. Montagu Williams's recollections may not have been as accurate as he would have liked, for there were many who felt that through his astute closing speech he had aided a murderer in escaping real justice.

Chapter 7

The Man Who Wasn't Jack the Ripper 1888

It is a mystery which will now probably never be solved; who was Jack the Ripper? This Northampton suspect has been named as a candidate. Find out why he most certainly was not.

The crimes of the Victorian murderer Jack the Ripper continue, over a century later, to arouse chillling fear as the mysterious dark secret created around the pseudonym inspires countless books and theories. Some authors even proclaim themselves to be Ripper historians and experts. It's a curious juxtaposition: if they are truly experts, then why have they not yet positively identified the killer? I think if we remove the title 'expert' and replace it with 'critic' then this provides a more apt description of the group who proclaim themselves as experts. It seems to me that all these people tend to do is write critiques on new works or suspects, ultimately using them for their own benefit.

The world of 'Ripperology', as it is called, is a highly sensitive and political one, fuelled by speculation, sinister suspicions and downright untruths. At the last trawl through Ripper lore I believe that over one hundred suspects had been advanced, ranging from royalty right down to the fish-porter boyfriend of the last victim, who, I hasten to add, was first identified in a book I wrote in 1991. Since then, I have researched and learned more on the subject, not fanatically, but in a more measured and methodical manner than some authors and researchers might. I still strongly suspect and believe Joseph Barnett to be the murderer of the last victim, Mary Jane Kelly. However, I now believe in addition that the Ripper crimes were linked, not by the police, but by the press. It's more than likely, then, that there were three, or perhaps four, separate and totally unconnected murders, which accounted for the press-fuelled hysteria that became the Jack the Ripper series of murders.

It was shortly after the publication of my book that I was invited to the USA to discuss the history of the crimes with FBI serial-killer profilers in Quantico, Virginia. During my trip to the States I went on countless radio shows to talk about my opinions regarding the latest theory proposed by an American writer, Dr David Abrahamsen, who had published a book naming James Kenneth Stephen as Jack the Ripper. What interested me more about this theory, and that is all it ever could be, was that Stephen died in the county where I lived, Northamptonshire.

Here, then, is the story of the man who most definitely was not Jack the Ripper and the fanciful theory which ended with his death in a Northampton hospital.

James Kenneth Stephen, often called 'Jem' by his friends and family, was born on 25 February 1859 in London. He was the second son of Judge Sir James Fitzjames Stephen and Mary Richenda Cunningham. His family had originally come from humble roots, but through hard work, dedication and determination they rose to grand societal heights. As well as his father, his brother Herbert and two uncles, James and Leslie, were also knighted, the latter being the father of the brilliant writer Virginia Woolf, who was Jem's first cousin. In his formative years Jem apparently struck up a relationship with a student from Eton, a boy who was three years his junior. This same student, Arthur C. Benson, would later, in 1911, publish his writing about Stephen and how he surrounded himself with young boys and enjoyed close and emotional relationships. In 1878, Stephen progressed to King's College, Cambridge, where he gained a Batchelor of Arts degree in 1882.

It is claimed that in 1883 he was allegedly recommended to act as a tutor to Prince Albert Victor during the Prince's formal residence at Cambridge. Jem without doubt abused this position and hand-picked Prince Albert Victor's social and academic friends. Prince Eddy, as he was known, was gradually introduced to the same circle of friends that Jem had and also into his interest groups.

By 1884, James Kenneth Stephen was called to the Bar, but

The man who wasn't Jack the Ripper.

remained as tutor and close friend and confidant to the Prince. It was when Eddy left Cambridge in 1885 that the relationship ended and Jem accepted a fellowship at the University. He remained at Cambridge and was a regular feature-writer in such notable publications as *The Pall Mall Gazette*, *The Saturday Recorder* and *The St James Gazette*. His time at Cambridge University ended somewhat abruptly in 1886, when he suffered an accident in Felixstowe. While he was out riding his horse during a holiday, the animal shied backwards throwing him into one of the blades of a windmill, which cut the back of his head. Indeed, other versions state that he was in fact trying to climb the windmill and accidentally caught his head on one of the propellers. In another he rode into a low-hanging tree bough, which knocked him clean off his horse, whereon he sustained the head injury.

Whatever the cause of the accident, it seems that there was a belief that mental illness would ensue. There was already a history of mental illness in his family, particularly in the male Stephens. Sir James had suffered a breakdown in 1885, which ultimately led to insanity. Jem, though, recovered from his illness during 1887.

After his period of convalescence he returned to his writing and founded his own newspaper, which he also edited. *The Reflector* was first published in 1888. The paper itself was intended to provide an intelligent and serious insight into any number of serious subjects, including politics, the literary world and, more defiantly, to stoke social consciences about poverty and deprivation across London, a subject which many other newspapers ignored, or at least, wouldn't dare discuss. Its first issue met with a flurry of interest. However, it struggled to sustain readership in a competitive market where people simply wanted to read the news and not any kind of morally questioning and academic insight into the world. Seventeen issues later, on 21 April, to be precise, *The Reflector* ceased to trade. Some of Stephen's close friends believed that *The Reflector* and his writings clearly displayed signs of his mental instability. A keen poet, one such verse penned by Jem clearly shows a hatred of women.

If all the harm that women have done,
Were put in a bottle and rolled into one,
Earth would not hold it,
The sky could not enfold it,
It could not be lighted nor warmed by the sun;
Such masses of evil
Would puzzle the Devil,
And keep him in fuel while Time's wheels run.
But if all the harm that's been done by men
Were doubled and doubled and doubled again,
And melted and fused into vapour and then
Were squared and raised to the power of ten,
There wouldn't be nearly enough, not near,
To keep a small girl for the tenth of a year.

The demise of his newspaper left Jem verging on depression. His father, perhaps recognising that his son was in a downward spiral, stepped in to provide support by way of offering him an opportunity to act as Clerk of the Assize, South Wales circuit during the summer of 1888. The role hardly inspired Jem; it is possible his father offered it to him in the vain hope that it would rekindle his desire to practise law. If that was the case then it failed, as he resigned from the position in

1890, whereon he returned to Cambridge to lecture and teach.

Now we come to the critical time in his life. It has been alleged by a number of proponents that, jilted and spurned by Eddy and entering the early stages of insanity during this period, he elected to embark on a crusade to embarrass the royal family and Prince Eddy. This he supposedly achieved by murdering and butchering common prostitutes in the East End to highlight the social deficiencies of Whitechapel.

This theory was first offered by Michael Harrison in his book *Clarence* (1972). The main thrust of the argument was based on the premise that Stephen and Prince Eddy had become homosexual lovers, either during or after Clarence's time at Cambridge. Harrison, seemingly quite correctly, identified that some of Stephen's verse indicated misogyny and clear messages that displayed sadistic tendencies. In further, even greater supposition, he then suggests that, once the affair was finished, in a vicious attempt to hurt his ex-lover, Stephen killed prostitutes on key dates that were significant to the royal family. Seemingly birthdays and pre-Christian religious festivals were selected for the murders. This all sounds reasonable enough, but research and factual data indicates that the only significant murders associated with the Jack the Ripper crimes which actually took place on such significant dates were: Martha Tabram, who, in all probability was not a victim of Jack the Ripper, but of a soldier. Tabram was murdered on the birthday of the Duke of Edinburgh; Mary Ann Nichols, who is generally believed to be the first canonical victim of the Ripper, was killed on the birthday of Princess Wilhelmina of the Netherlands and was potentially killed by Charles Andrew Cross or Robert Paul; Mary Jane Kelly was killed on the birthday of the Prince of Wales, by Joseph Barnett, as I said earlier.

Factually, for whatever reason, the mental state of James Kenneth Stephen appeared to deteriorate in or around 1890. This fits in reasonably well with the Ripper suspect theory, until finally on 21 November 1891, his brother Herbert, knowing the dark secret about his brother, took him to St Andrew's Hospital, Northampton, where he died on 3 February 1892. He furiously resisted the notion that his mind had given way at the end of his life.

In support of this case, it was further suggested in a letter to the

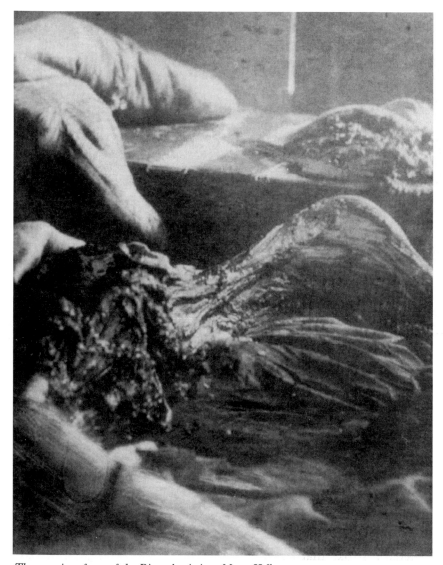

The remains of one of the Ripper's victims, Mary Kelly.

Sunday Times in the mid-1970s, by a Mrs Marny Halam, that her great-grandfather, who had been a barrister, informed the family that the authorities apparently knew who the Ripper was – it was James Kenneth Stephen! *Fait accompli.*

Indeed, over the years, many authors have depicted Stephen as

St Andrew's Hospital, Northampton, where Ripper suspect J. K. Stephen died.

playing an integral role in the Ripper murders. Not all have him as the sole protagonist. In the majority he is but an accomplice. Dr David Abrahamsen had him working right alongside the Duke of Clarence (Eddy) introducing whores to the Prince and killing them at will. The theme of this theory was that Eddy was syphilitic and suffered from brain disease, which caused him to kill the prostitutes from whom he had contracted the disease. There was also a link to Queen Victoria's surgeon, Sir William Withey Gull, who is also a latter-day suspect for the murders, despite the fact that he was in his seventies and had suffered a stroke that left one side of his body with slight paralysis. Then there are the theories of John Wilding, who in his book *Jack the Ripper Revealed* actually links Jem with a legal fellow in the form of struggling barrister, Montague J. Druitt. Supporting this is the fact that Druitt later committed suicide in the River Thames, seemingly through guilt and remorse.

So, returning to the subject of my radio interviews in America. I rapidly read through the Abrahamsen book and disagreed with its approach. It was a regurgitation of what was already known, with one difference, the good doctor had been to Northampton and had been given access to the Stephen medical case notes from St Andrew's Hospital of 1891/1892 which, he claimed, stated that he was Jack the Ripper! I confess to feeling mortified. There I was in America, discussing the criminal profiling of Joseph Barnett, which had significant peaks and accents to make him a serious contender for a killer, when in the county where I policed and lived the identity of Jack the Ripper had apparently lain hidden for over one hundred years. I desperately yearned to speak with the doctor. Sadly I never got the opportunity, for he refused to appear on any of the shows with me. I wondered why. Why should he opt not to do so when he possessed such damning and positive evidence against James Kenneth Stephen?

Returning home, I made contact with St Andrew's Hospital and met senior practising staff to discuss the contents of the Abrahamsen book. In no time I had ascertained many things, not least of which was the fact that the information relating to the doctor who Abrahamsen claimed had given him access to the notes, was, to put it mildly, grossly inaccurate. Thereafter, some of the medical notes and, in particular, those that made reference to Jack the Ripper simply didn't exist.

It was then that I realised why the good doctor wouldn't appear on the radio with me: he perhaps believed that I then knew the detailed inaccuracies his book contained.

So there the Northampton link to the crimes of Jack the Ripper ends. James Kenneth Stephen did die in a Northampton hospital in 1892, but he most certainly wasn't one of the fiends who killed whores in Whitechapel during a few weeks in 1888.

Finally, it would be remiss of me not to mention that the county of Northamptonshire did actually have a somewhat tenuous connection with the murder investigation into this series of crimes, in the form of Chief Inspector Frederick Abberline, whose wife, Martha (née Mackness), died of consumption in 1868 in the then Northamptonshire village of Elton.

Chapter 8

A Sad Love Affair
1892

*A married man tracks his lover from one end
of the country to the other. Once he loved her: now
he needs to rid himself of her. How?*

Murder of any sort is an abhorrent act and one which is unforgivable. As we clamour to understand what drives one person to end the life of another, every so often one can research a crime which evokes no rational explanation other than to bolster the killer's own sense of self-worth and feeling of control. Richard Sabey is one such killer. Born in the village of Cranfield in Bedfordshire in 1845, it has to be said that he was a reasonably intelligent man. Given a decent upbringing by morally good parents, he was taught the difference between right and wrong behaviour. As he grew through his adolescent years he enlisted in the British Army and was at once called up for active service in such places as India and Africa. During one such spell in India, Sabey met and married an Indian woman. He carried out a full term of service then returned to England along with his new spouse and a child. The family settled in Leicester.

Sabey now faced problems of a different nature, identifying and finding suitable employment to support his wife and family and maintain the marital home. As a confident young man who possessed excellent communication skills he knew he had the ability to talk himself into work.

The Bedford Gas company was very soon his new employer. The company needed staff to carry out a variety of roles and Sabey soon found himself the postholder of one such position. Despite his somewhat gregarious personality, the sad fact about Richard Sabey was that he was an inveterate liar; he had an inbuilt need to impress everyone he met, particularly members of the opposite sex. At work he was disliked by many of his contemporaries whom, on every occasion, he tried to outshine. His lies and deceitful ways made him grossly unpopular yet this mattered little to him; he simply couldn't stop himself. Time and again Sabey would recount tales of his sexual exploits with the company's female customers, whom he would visit at their homes while their husbands were at work. Generally speaking, it was household staff with whom he more commonly associated, women who were more vulnerable to his lies and devious ways and would fall prey to his disingenuous manner.

Shortly, Sabey was called to a large house in the village of Cranfield to carry out some work, and while there he became friendly with a pretty young housemaid by the name of Louisa Sophia Johnson, who also hailed from the village. Louise had not experienced the ways of the world and was rather naïve; she fell for Sabey's flattery and apparent charm. He uttered lie after lie as he showered the young woman with cheap gifts and gave her false promises and all the desired attention necessary to get his wicked way with her. He never once explained to her that he was in fact a married man with a child. So began a sexually tempestuous and torrid affair, which was, from the outset, destined to end in abject failure. Sabey was able to convince Louisa that his continued absences from Cranfield were due to his irregular work patterns; the reality was that he was returning home to Leicester to his wife and child. As for his wife, she received the same explanation, work patterns dictating his forced absence from the family home.

It wasn't very long before Louisa fell pregnant with Sabey's child. Loyal to her lover, she refused to reveal the identity of the illegitimate child's father, but most people knew it to be Richard Sabey. After the baby's birth, Sabey more or less abandoned the Louisa, though it has be said that this was, in the main, forced on him by the hostility of local people, who held a strong belief that he was the cad who had caused the situation. Within days of suffering both verbal and physical abuse, Sabey voluntarily opted to leave the area.

Being an extremely devious man, to the local people who threatened him, he stood as a man of his word, claiming that he would now leave the young woman and her newborn child alone, yet secretly he made arrangements with Louisa for her to resign from her position of employment and to travel with him to Liverpool where they could live together. Foolishly, Louisa did as Sabey asked.

Soon the couple were moving into rooms owned by a Mrs Peacock in the Liverpool area; this was at a rental cost of five shillings per week. From the outset, the landlady appeared to be most sympathetic towards Louisa's plight. She had seen enough dodgy characters coming through her rooms in her time to recognise another one, and there was no doubt in her mind that Richard Sabey was one such individual.

In truth, Mrs Peacock acted as a surrogate mother to the young woman and the child, caring for her and giving 'motherly' advice about how to provide to the needs of a young baby as and when necessary.

Sabey, Johnson and their child lived together ostensibly quite happily for a few days until Sabey announced that work was going to force him to return to the Midlands for a few days. He assured his lover that he would be back as soon as he could. Despite this assurance, Louisa felt extremely vulnerable but agreed that money was necessary to keep a roof over their heads and for the upbringing of the child. Little did Louisa realise that in reality this was the beginning of an ongoing situation in which Sabey would flit between his legal home and family in Leicester and his secret life in Liverpool. Twice a week he would literally swap homes, telling more and more lies to both women to cover his tracks.

After a few weeks the stress began to take its toll on Sabey. His 'Walter Mitty' lifestyle was beginning to fall apart at the seams; for one thing he couldn't cope financially with running two homes and raising two separate families. His life was a complete sham, a masquerade where he where he took centre-stage: two women and two families, to whom he constantly lied. The deceit became increasingly harder to cover up, and cracks began to appear in his stories as both women gradually became suspicious about his away-from-home activities.

The pressure eventually forced Sabey to breaking-point and during one visit to his Leicester home he found himself cornered by his wife's interrogation. Desperate, he blurted out the truth of the extra-marital affair and his double existence to his wife.

Mrs Sabey did not take kindly to the news and instructed her husband to end the illicit relationship in Liverpool at once. From all the evidence available, and judging by the type of character he was, it seems certain that Sabey blamed Louisa for the affair, portraying her as a scarlet woman who spotted his vulnerability and seized on the opportunity to fleece him for her own advantage.

Early in the morning of 29 November 1892, Mrs Sabey arrived in Liverpool and without warning turned up at the rooms of Mrs Peacock. There she demanded to speak with Louisa. Inside the house, Louisa had no idea what was happening when the Indian wife of her beloved Richard Sabey entered the room and launched into a tirade of abuse, accusing her of encouraging her husband into an illicit relationship. The young woman stood sobbing hysterically, unable to find an answer or escape from the abuse being thrown at her. Meanwhile, Richard Sabey, forever weak and an undeniable coward, stood behind his wife, supporting her and allowing her to emotionally destroy Louisa. Every so often he would speak up, backing his wife's claims and calling Louisa some nasty names and pretending that he had been the naïve one, but overall displaying united animosity at what she had done to him. Running out of expletives and seeing that young Louisa was now mentally broken, Mrs Sabey screamed at her, 'Remember, I am here now and if I catch you about with Dick again I shall give you a good hiding.' More incredibly, she followed up this comment to Louisa with an instruction for her to dress the child of the illicit relationship, pack all its things together and hand it over to her for adoption so that she and Richard could raise it, thus destroying all evidence of any affair! As any good mother would, Louisa refused and, seeking some temporary peace, requested, with Mrs Peacock's help, that they both leave her alone at once, which they did.

Mrs Peacock was as supportive as anyone could be, but she had a business to run and it wasn't long before she asked for her rent money, which Louisa obviously couldn't provide. With a heavy heart, Mrs Peacock had to ask Louisa and her child to leave the rooms as soon as possible, but she did not simply turn her out onto the streets. She was decent enough to help Louisa find accommodation in a Liverpool workhouse, although the conditions were hardly conducive to the raising of a healthy baby.

In December of the same year, Louisa gave birth to a second child as a result of the former relationship with Sabey. The poor child was born in the workhouse. Depressed and alone, Louisa continued in a downward spiral and when, in January 1893, her first child contracted an illness and died, it seemed things could get no worse.

The loss left the young woman feeling truly devastated; she had no one to whom she could turn. She had to get out of the damp and miserable environment of the workhouse, but how? In a desperate attempt to free herself and give her remaining child a chance of a decent life she wrote to her sister in Northamptonshire. Unlike Louisa, her sister had married a respectable man and a reliable worker by the name of Thomas Frederick Wright. Together the couple lived in picturesque surroundings, at Isebrook Cottage, between Burton Latimer and Finedon. It was an idyllic location, and the River Ise flowed past the end of its garden. The two sisters soon engaged in written communication and before long Louisa found herself guided by her sibling. The first thing Louisa was told to do was to take out an affiliation summons against Dick Sabey, thus forcing him into making some financial contribution towards the child's upbringing. The result as that Sabey was ordered to pay three shillings and sixpence a week to Louisa. The summons and respective order caused more than financial hardship in the Sabey household: it acted as a permanent reminder to his wife of her husband's infidelity, something for which she quite properly made him suffer.

With life now seeming to offer much more promise, Louisa accepted the invitation to move to Isebrook Cottage to stay with her sister and her family for a time, at least until such time as she was fully recuperated and able to find employment and sufficient funds to be able to support herself, and a place to live. What a world of difference this must have made to Louisa and her child, from the confines of a dark and dingy Liverpool workhouse to the gorgeous rural surroundings of a sleepy Northamptonshire hollow.

Back in Leicester, Dick Sabey was beginning to find his life unbearable. His wife didn't trust him at all and allowed him little room for manoeuvre or flexibility. The mistrust festered and at times turned into violent quarrels and verbal abuse. Deep inside, Sabey was looking for an opportunity for escape. He believed that Louisa would still be passionately in love with him and that he could win her over without any real effort. It was of course a truly false perception, born from the deluded mind of a desperate man who had fallen victim to a pattern of deceit woven by himself. Dick Sabey was in fact the last person Louisa wanted to see; he had broken her heart once, and she would not let him do it again.

Spinning his wife a pack of lies, Sabey once again explained that his work was going to take him away for a few days. In reality he was taking a trip north to visit Louisa. On 6 February 1893 he left his Leicester home for the journey to Mrs Peacock's lodging-house in Liverpool. At the back of his mind were the extra outgoings he was being forced to pay to Louisa through the affiliation order. If he could persuade Louisa to drop this he would be financially better off. Furthermore, he was arrogant enough to believe that he could have one further sexual encounter with Louisa before finally ending the relationship and leaving her behind for good. His mindset was fixed and he had nothing to lose and everything to gain.

Arriving in the Merseyside city, he made his way to the rooms of Mrs Peacock and was alarmed to find that Louisa had moved out and into the local workhouse a few months previously. The fact that she had apparently made a decision for herself and was perhaps making a new life for herself angered him. It meant she could have met another man who would show Sabey to be what he was: a self-centred and weak man. Undeterred, he made his way to the workhouse and asked staff if he could speak to Louisa. The response was, of course, not what he anticipated; he was told the woman had left the city to go to live with her sister in Burton Latimer. This news left him feeling betrayed and seething. How dare Louisa make a life for herself without his guidance? His control over the young woman was slipping. Now it was he who was out of control.

Staying overnight in Liverpool, he visited a hardware shop and purchased a sharp-bladed knife. The following morning he began his journey to Northamptonshire to track down Louisa with only one thing on his mind: murder.

The location where the killer Sabey hid in the road before meeting Louisa Johnson.

Arriving in Northampton a couple of days later, Sabey could find no trace of Isebrook Cottage and it took him many hours to locate it, but he eventually did. The coward in him meant that he was scared to approach it for fear of confrontation with the man of the house. Instead he opted to hide behind a hedgerow on the side of the road and watched the house in the hope that Louisa would emerge alone. Before long, Louisa walked out of the house and into Finedon Road, which ran close to its boundary wall. She was carrying an empty pail in which she was going to collect fresh water from Burton Mill. Sabey's heart began to pound with excited anticipation. He watched as Louisa carefully filled the pail and began her return journey to the house. As she passed close to him, he stepped out from his hiding place and spoke to her. Whatever was said between the pair, it appears that he quelled her wariness sufficiently for him to be able to walk some of the journey alongside the young woman without her objecting.

A local baker, Edward Partridge, called at Isebrook Cottage at around the same time as Sabey and Louisa's encounter. He stated that he saw the man (Sabey) place his arm around the girl in a casual and relaxed manner; he believed the couple looked perfectly relaxed in each other's company.

Walking behind the couple, he met local ironstone workers, William and John Evans and James Burley. The group thought nothing of the couple ahead of them until suddenly they saw the man (Sabey) grab the woman (Johnson) by the throat, forcing her head back. With his free hand he calmly produced a knife and sliced it deep into the woman's throat, severing the carotid artery as he did so. Blood spurted

It was at this site where Louisa Sophia Johnson was cruelly murdered by Richard Sabey.

from the woman's throat as she somehow managed to scream the words, 'Murder! He's trying to kill me!' She then fell from the man's grasp, taking a few steps towards the local workers before collapsing in a vast pool of crimson-red blood, which gushed from the gaping wound in her throat.

Sabey panicked and disappeared behind a hedgerow into a field owned by a Mr Barlow. Meanwhile, Thomas Wright came out of his home, wondering what all the commotion was about. There he saw Louisa lying in the road and at once ran to her. Picking her up, he carried her back to Isebrook Cottage, where he laid her on a bed and she died.

Outside, James Burley ran after Sabey and demanded that he come out from behind the hedgerow. The cowardly killer pleaded for the man not to harm him and slowly emerged. He refused to give up the bloodstained knife and at one point held it in front of him, threatening to use it against anyone who came near him. Thomas Wright approached the group and walked up to the knife-wielding man, whom he realised must be Dick Sabey. 'Well, Mr Wright, she did it!' shouted Sabey. 'That's a lie, Dick!' exclaimed Wright. Sabey then yelled out, 'Love did it!' He reached into his pocket and looked Thomas Wright in the eye, holding out his hand he offered him a sovereign. Thomas sneered at him and told him he didn't want his dirty money. Sabey began to cry and requested that he Thomas send it on to his wife in Leicester; Thomas agreed, and in the process took the opportunity to take possession of the knife as well.

Sabey, sobbing, told the men who now surrounded him that he had intended to kill Louisa and then do away with himself, but they had prevented him from fulfilling this. There was not one of the men present who actually believed this statement. He was terrified of suffering a beating by his captors: such a man would not be capable of doing away with himself.

Soon a horse-drawn bus came along and was duly stopped by the men. The driver was told to take them to the Constable in Finedon; they had a murderer they wished to deliver to him. The bus carried the group to the *Gate Inn*, near Finedon, where they alighted and entered the hostelry. Inside, Sabey pulled out money and purchased his captors a round of beer while they awaited the arrival of the Constable.

Constable William Judge soon arrived at the pub and spoke with the witnesses, listening to their story. He at once arrested Richard Sabey for murder. Sabey denied killing Louisa and instead blamed 'undying love for the girl' for the resultant action. The response had little impact on Judge. To him the facts were simple and straightforward: a woman had been killed and it was Sabey who had deliberately taken her life. The Constable advised the prisoner that he would be taken to Northampton jail, where he would be detained until his trial.

The body of Louisa Sophia Johnson was removed from Isebrook Cottage and taken to the *Red Cow* public house, less than a mile distant, in Burton Latimer, where a post-mortem took place. The cause of death was confirmed as a result of severance of the carotid artery – Louisa had effectively bled to death. Her funeral took place in the cemetery in Church Lane, Burton Latimer. It was reported that a crowd of 1,500 mourners attended, crammed into the tiny area of consecrated ground. The remains of Louisa Sophia Johnson were interred close to the tiny cemetery's main gates. Today it can be found nestling protected beneath a large tree. An iron memorial tablet stands at the head of the grave. Now sadly broken, it reads:

In affectionate remembrance of
Louisa Sophia Johnson of Cranfield Bedfordshire.
Died 8 February 1893 aged twenty eight years.
The Lord has brought down my strength in my journey
and shortened my days.

Richard Sabey was brought to trial at the Northampton assizes in July 1893. His confession and admission of guilt eased the burden of responsibility on the gathered court officials and he was quickly found guilty of murder and two days later hanged at Northampton.

Typically, on the morning of his execution a large crowd had gathered outside the prison walls. Ballads were chanted and penny broadsheets depicting the crime were sold to those keen to learn the sad details of the crime. Among the crowd stood one woman, who remained silent and seemingly dispassionate about proceedings. As the black flag was hoisted, signifying that Sabey had been dispatched, the crowd screamed its joy that another ruthless and despicable killer had left this Earth. Those who took the time to look at the lonely woman

The victim's grave.

may have noticed a steady flow of tears streaming down her cheeks. She turned and moved away from the crowd and made the relatively short trip back to her home in Leicester. Mrs Sabey had lost a husband. However, it was also a release from the living hell she had endured for so long with a deceitful man.

Chapter 9

The East Haddon Mystery
1892

*What really happened to a wonderful mother and
child in Northampton? Murder and an awful
lot of mystery.*

There are some crimes of murder that are more grotesque and unpalatable than others. Every so often we are gripped by the amount or type of violence portrayed in the act, so much so that it arouses our deepest emotions, making us despise the killer or the violator. We conjure up images of the perpetrator in our own minds, depicting him or her as a living symbol representing evil, a devil incarnate, if you like. The crime I am about to discuss possesses all the sanguinary 'delights' to titillate the tastebuds of the most ardent true-crime reader. Sadly, it happened in Northampton and still leaves a bitter taste indeed. Often referred to as the 'Bacon Warehouse murder', this crime is of the foulest sort.

The year was 1892. Her Majesty Queen Victoria was on the throne, and policing in England was not generally regarded as a respectable occupation. The murders by Jack the Ripper in Whitechapel, London, just four years earlier had tarnished the reputation of the police. Furthermore, more bodies had been discovered in the East End of London and the murders seemed to bear some resemblance to those of the Ripper: mutilation of a female. Headless and limbless torsos had been found in London, yet the maniacal killer was never brought to justice. For the average reader of the Victorian penny dreadful newspaper such crimes could only occur in the metropolis. They could never happen in the leafy rural environment of such places as Northampton, or could they?

I leave the reporting of this case to the press of the day, who reported the entire proceedings relating to what undoubtedly was a double murder:

The last sad scene in connection with the what has since been known as 'The East Haddon Mystery' was enacted this morning in Her Majesty's Prison, Northampton, when Andrew George McRae, who was on Christmas Eve last convicted of the murder of Annie Pritchard and sentenced to death by Mr Justice Kennedy, suffered the extreme penalty of the law at the hands of Billington, the Public Executioner. On the morning of Sunday, 7th August last year (1892) the town was first startled by the announcement that the remains of a human body had been found in a ditch on the turnpike road about half a mile from Althorp Park station, on the road to East Haddon and Long Buckby. They were wrapped in some sacking or wrappering, and were also partially clothed. At first it was thought the remains were those of a dead sheep or some other animal, but on closer examination they were found to be those of a human body in a shockingly advanced state of decomposition, so much so that on being moved what was left of the body fell from the bones, and the latter also fell to pieces. Upon a subsequent examination the remains were found to be those of a young woman, partially clothed, and that the body was headless and armless, only the trunk and the legs remaining, the latter being tied to the buttocks. The shocking discovery became the subject of considerable comment, both in the town and in the county, as it was thought that none other than a most diabolical murder had been committed and this conjecture subsequently proved to be correct.

An inquest was held on the remains on Tuesday, 9th August and adjourned for a month, and ultimately what might be termed practically an open verdict of 'Found Dead' was returned. On the wrappering a label bearing the name of E.M. McRae was discovered, though but little weight was attached to the fact at the time, as Mr E.M. McRae who was at that time a bacon factor having a stall in the Northampton market and a warehouse in Dychurch Lane gave evidence at the inquest and explained that he at times sold wrappers of such a character to many different classes of people. The shocking discovery was taken up by both the County and Borough police, but as they had so little to work upon nothing could be elucidated to in any way to enable them to attempt to solve the mystery. Having that label in view, they, however, continued to work with some amount of success. The news of the supposed horrible murder soon spread throughout the town and county by means of the local press and also

The Red Lion *inn, where the body was taken and the inquest took place.*

throughout the country. The remains were at first thought to be those of a Miss Tite who had been missed by her mother for some time and a skirt in which they were encased was partially identified by the mother as being similar to that her daughter was wearing when she left home. This however proved to be groundless and ultimately Miss Tite returned to Northampton safe and well.

Fortunate circumstances occurred, which on being well worked out by the County and Borough police, threw considerable light on the matter and in the end led to an arrest. After the lapse of some three weeks or a month, information was given by a Mrs Bland, a dealer in second hand clothes, residing in College Street, Northampton, that Andrew George McRae, the brother of E.M. McRae, had sold her several articles of a woman's apparel and also some baby linen in the latter part of the month of July. Andrew George McRae was then seen by the Police and in reply to their questions as to how he came to be dealing with the clothes, volunteered certain answers. McRae, who was 36 years of age, was, at that time working for his brother as an assistant at the stall on Market Square, and also had charge of the warehouse in Dychurch Lane of which he kept the keys. He was a married man, lodging in Northampton, but had a wife and two young sons residing in Birmingham. His answers to the questions put to him with reference to his dealing with the clothes caused a reference to be made to the wife in Birmingham, without the knowledge of McRae; and his statements were found to be untrue. He was also closely questioned as to the label and said the only account he could give of it was that it must have been attached to the wrappers in which his brother received bacon from London, some of which were disposed of. Further enquiries were then instituted by the Police and on Saturday, 3rd September McRae was arrested on suspicion of murdering a woman unknown. In reply to the charge he sad 'I am innocent.' He was brought before the County Magistrates on Monday, 5th September and remanded till Saturday, 10th September. Prior to his arrest and between that time and the prisoner being brought up on remand the Police had made enquiries in Birmingham and found out that a young woman named Annie Pritchard left her home in the previous March and had not been heard of since. A family of the name of Pritchard resided near the house of the man Andrew George McRae, in Birmingham. It transpired that he had been on the most intimate terms with Annie Pritchard, a young woman about the age of 32 years, in fact on terms of such intimacy as to cause the matter to be adverted to in strong terms of disappropriation by the members of the Pritchard family.

On the young woman leaving Birmingham she led her sisters and brothers to believe she was going to Liverpool to be married to a man named Guy Anderson, a lithographic artist with whom it was said she had previously been in company in Birmingham, and then they were going to America. On her departure from Birmingham she took with her some two or three large and small boxes, containing a quantity of clothing and other articles, among the latter of which were certain family relics. Instead of going to Liverpool, however, it was asserted she came to Northampton and lived with the man McRae in St John Street under the name of Mr and Mrs Anderson, until July 20th when they left.

In June the supposed Mrs Anderson gave birth to a child and was attended to by a midwife and other persons. On the evening of 20th

July Mr Anderson (McRae) and Mrs Anderson (the alleged Annie Pritchard) left St John Street with the supposed intention of going to fresh lodgings in Derby Road. They were accompanied to the top of Bridge Street by a young woman named Elliott who carried the baby, where they parted, McRae stating that they could manage without her assistance any further. He also stated they were going to the post office and that they could take the tram thence to their new lodgings. From that night, however, neither the woman nor the child have ever been seen and it is conjectured they were both murdered that night in the warehouse in Dychurch Lane. After the finding of the remains of the woman in the ditch and the inquest having been held, the clothing was removed and kept by the police.

The remains were subsequently buried in the new cemetery at East Haddon and were the first interment there. The funeral was attended by a large number of persons, the ceremony being conducted by the Rev Mr Ruston, Congregational minister for Long Buckby. Shortly afterwards, by public subscription a memorial stone was raised over the grave of the unfortunate victim. A portion of the clothing in which the remains were wrapped was subsequently identified by the sister of Annie Pritchard as belonging to her and as having been taken away with her when she left Birmingham. She was also shown the other clothes and articles which McRae had been found disposing of and identified them as her sister's property, as also did her brother John. The police, both of the County and the Borough, to their great credit were also able to forge a very strong chain of circumstantial evidence against McRae in many other particulars, and it was fully believed they had secured the murderer of Annie Pritchard.

At the adjourned hearing before the Magistrates the facts above related were adduced and at a further adjourned hearing on 19th and 20th September the prisoner, who stood charged with the murder of Annie Pritchard, and who was defended by Mr C.C. Becke was fully committed for trial. It transpired during the latter hearing that a letter supposed to have been written from Liverpool by Annie Pritchard to her sister at Birmingham, stating that she was then going to be married to Guy Anderson and was then going to America was given to a commercial traveller by her at the Castle Station to post at Liverpool, which he did.

Strong circumstantial evidence was also given in other ways as to

Annie Pritchard's grave, tucked away from the main cemetery area.

McRae's actions while at the warehouse in Dychurch Lane and to his having taken a dog cart on two occasions on 26th July for the purpose, it was asserted of removing the remains to where they were found deposited.

The assizes were opened in Northampton on 16 November and on the morning of the 17th the trial of Andrew George McRae for the wilful murder of Annie Pritchard was proceeded with and it was thought singular that nothing as to the murder of the child was mentioned in the indictment. It should be stated that neither the head, nor arms of the woman, or the body of the child have been able *to be found or in any way accounted for.*

The hearing of the charge was proceeded with before Mr Justice Kennedy who had taken his first circuit as a Judge. Mr M.C. Buzzard, QC, with Mr Ryland D. Adkins appeared for the prosecution on behalf of the treasury. The prisoner was defended by Mr Walter A. Attenborough and Mr Hammond Chambers. The prisoner on being placed in the dock was naturally regarded with the closest attention. He, however, walked briskly into the dock and did not show any signs of feeling the position in which he was placed or the ultimate result which might follow. The case proceeded up to lunch time.

While the Police officer was being sworn as bailiff to take charge of the Jury during their retirement, a Juryman (Mr J. Asplin of Milton) left the box and proceeded to his hostelry to fetch, as he subsequently stated, an important letter which was in his overcoat pocket. In the meantime the other jurymen were taken to their room and the absence of Mr Asplin was noticed. A police officer went in search of him and he was found in the street about 25 minutes afterwards. The fact was reported to counsel and then to the judge. Counsel was invited to meet the Judge to discuss the position. Ultimately, the Judge decided to postpone the hearing of the case to the next assizes and the next morning fined the juryman £50 which, notwithstanding an appeal to the Treasury he had to pay. During the hearing his Lordship on appeal reconsidered his decision as to postponing the case to the next assizes and ultimately stated he would return at the conclusion of the Warwickshire Assizes and proceed with the trial on 20 December, for which the prisoner thanked his Lordship. It now meant a wait from 18 November to 20 December.

At the subsequent trial the chain of circumstantial evidence against the prisoner was forged link by link with no less than 47 witnesses being examined by the prosecution. It was shown that the prisoner had been dealing with wearing apparel known to have belonged to Annie Pritchard, that he had told contradictory and untrue statements as to her whereabouts, that he had purchased lime (lime having been discovered on the body when found), that charred fragments of bone, which were said to be those of a human hand had been found under the copper in the warehouse in Dychurch Lane and that in the copper there was a greasy fluid in which there was human hair.

The copper where the remains of the missing baby were burned.

The main line of the defence was that there was no evidence to show that the remains were those of Annie Pritchard and that she had probably gone off with Guy Anderson who might have been the father of her child. The trial continued for five full days. Mr Buzzard took three hours in his closing speech and the closing speech by Mr Attenborough for the defence took five hours. Similarly on Christmas Eve Mr Justice Kennedy took five hours with his final instructions and speech to the jury. So it was that on Christmas Eve the jury deliberated for one and half hours before returning with a guilty verdict. The prisoner was asked if had anything he wanted to say. He said that any sentence passed on him had no terror for him because he was perfectly innocent of the charge made against him. He turned

Annie Pritchard with her lover and murderer, Andrew George McRae.

to the jury and added; 'Each and every one of you this day has become what you have made me – a murderer, you have widowed a good devoted wife and made fatherless loving children. Go to your homes with clear consciences if you can, for as long as you live your consciences will accuse you.' Mr Justice Kennedy then sentenced him to hang by the neck until he was dead. McRae pushed back his shoulders and stood erect, almost to attention, he displayed no emotion whatsoever.

Right up to the end he protested his innocence. Contrary to the wishes of the Governor of the Prison the press were issued with four cards of admission – two to London journalists and two to local pressmen. The reporters were admitted to the waiting room on the North side of the prison yard at 8.20 a.m. and at a quarter to nine the bell of St Sepulchre began to toll. A few minutes before nine McRae who had slept well and eaten a hearty breakfast submitted calmly to the ordeal of pinioning at the hands of Billington, after which the procession started for the scaffold. The Rev. W. Phillips, reading the sentences of the service for the Burial of the Dead, in a clear, impassive voice. McRae walked firmly to his doom with his head erect.

At the point where the reporters joined the procession, the condemned man turned his head and bowed slightly. On the scaffold being reached, the strapping of the legs was but the work of a moment, and in the midst of the solemn recital of the words 'In the midst of life we are in death,' Billington pulled the lever and McRae disappeared, death being instantaneous.

An estimated 12,000 people had gathered outside the prison, those close to the South corner claimed to hear a distinct 'thud' when the body was dropped through the scaffold trap door.

McRae's wife, who was among those who had gathered outside the prison walls, turned and walked form the scene as the black flag was hoisted within the prison walls. Her head bowed, she knew that her husband had now departed this Earth, leaving behind a legacy of deceit and hurt that his family had to deal with for the rest of their days. McRae may go down on record as the most callous killer in Northamptonshire's history. However, he was without doubt the most cowardly. To kill a mother and her daughter, his own daughter, an innocent baby, defies belief, yet that is exactly what McRae did.

For the poor family of Annie Pritchard there was further pain, as not one of the local parishes wished to have her remains buried in the consecrated grounds of their parish. It took some high-powered intervention to resolve matters, and so Annie was buried at the new East Haddon graveyard. A collection was made and a decent headstone erected to mark her final resting place.

Chapter 10

Murder Without Motive
1901

*A turbulant on-off relationship results in one of the
most horrific murders in the country's history.*

Alexander Claydon, and his wife, Louisa, both aged forty-three, lived together in Portland Street, Northampton. At the rear of the home was Alex's workshop, where he crafted leather shoes and worked to earn a meagre living as a shoemaker. It has to be said that Alex much preferred drinking with his friends to working, and lacked the real discipline necessary to forge a decent income through his home-working.

It was the second time around for both Alexander and Louisa; both had been married previously and lost their partners to illness, though there is some suggestion that Louisa lost her husband through his addiction to alcohol. Alex and Louisa were married for just a few years before formally separating (confirmed by court legislation) in 1899. It was an acrimonious separation, and Alex had been taken back to court several times, on one occasion being jailed for failing to keep up maintenance payments.

Christmas 1900 saw the couple back together and Alex moving into the home with Louisa, his ten-year-old son and Kate Wareing, aged eighteen, who was Louisa's daughter from her first marriage. Initially Alex made real efforts at reparation and was keen to keep his wife and family happy, so made the extra effort to work and bring in money to help support the family. Louisa, meanwhile, did washing for other families, which brought in that little bit extra to allow Alex some financial freedom to socialise. Despite this industrious effort, theirs still wasn't a happy home; in fact, beneath the surface, it was filled with animosity and contempt. Kate Wareing didn't trust or like her step-father, especially the way he would at times speak to her mother, crudely and without care. In late June, once again the couple parted. Alex began to spend much of his time in a drunken stupor and was forced to sleep rough, often under hedgerows.

Louisa, it would seem, temporarily took pity on her husband and allowed him to return to the home for a short time. On Saturday, 6 July 1901, Alex went out in the early afternoon. As always, he refused to do any work, and demanded money from his wife. She refused, not by choice, but because she simply didn't have any for him to waste on alcohol. Despite this, Alex went down his local pub, the *Old Globe* on Kettering Road, and found his friends more than willing to subsidise and keep company with him. He left the pub shortly after 11.00 p.m. and made his way home, arriving there before midnight. Louisa was not impressed and told Alex that his behaviour was totally unacceptable and that he was destroying what little remained of their relationship through his unwillingness to support the family in any way. She then went to bed, leaving her husband silently seething downstairs. Alex was angry at his wife's reaction. Quite irrationally and unreasonably, he wondered how she dare treat him like this. How dare she pick him up and drop him at her own will? Surely, he thought, he was within his rights to go to the pub to socialise? He was the master of the home, he could come and go as he saw fit, and not only when his wife allowed him to!

It was around 2.00 a.m. on Sunday, 7 July when Alex struck his wife with a blow to the temple with his shoemaker's file (a 16-inch-long instrument with a sharp pointed end). Before the poor woman could do anything, he stuffed the corner of the quilt down her throat to prevent her from crying out for help. Then, with the sharpened end of the file, he proceeded to stab her repeatedly in the face before plunging it deep into her left breast. Louisa wasn't struggling any more; she was dead. As if these injuries weren't sufficient, to make sure he had completed his murderous task, he then took his shoemaker's awl and plunged it deep into her neck.

Leaving the carnage behind him, he went downstairs and helped himself to some bread and butter, which Louisa had prepared for him earlier, in his absence. He then returned to the bedroom, undressed and climbed into bed beside the motionless and bloodstained body of his dead wife, and fell asleep. When he awoke a few hours later, he saw the damage he had inflicted on his poor wife: the facial features were unrecognisable, her flesh had been ripped and torn apart, and congealed blood sat deep in the wounds. Horrified, he felt sick, and unable to look any longer at his savage butchery, he put a pillow over her face, got dressed and left the house.

After wandering the streets for a few hours, he eventually gave himself up to the unsuspecting and somewhat alarmed Constable Bailey at Moulton Police house. At around 10 a.m. Kate Wareing was entering her mother's bedroom when she saw the blood-splattered walls and bed sheets on which her mother's blood-saturated corpse lay. She stopped in her tracks and did not approach the bed; instead she ran down the stairs, out of the house and straight to *The Engineer* public house, where she raised the alarm with Susan Langley, the landlady.

Soon the police had been informed about the situation at the Claydon house. Chief Inspector Bates and Sub-Inspector Allen made their way to the murder scene. The gossip about the gruesome scene spread quickly, and thousands of sightseers gathered in the street outside the house. Through this communication, six other constables had been alerted and made their way to the house. Chief Inspector Bates viewed the scene and listened to what Kate Wareing had to say about the tempestuous relationship her mother had with her husband and Kate's step-father, Alex Claydon. There had been violence between the couple prior to the murder; Alex was quick to give his wife a slap to keep her in her place. It was clear from all Bates heard, not only from Kate but from neighbours, that the only suspect for the crime was Alex Claydon. The body of Louisa Claydon was removed to Northampton mortuary. Sergeant MacLeod was instructed to circulate the description and details of the wanted man (short, stout and with a dark, drooping moustache). None of the officers at the scene were aware at this stage that Alex Claydon was already under lock and key at Moulton.

Claydon was taken before the Mayor of Northampton, F. G. Adnitt, who presided over the hearing, and five other magistrates at the Guildhall. He seemed totally without remorse as the charge of murder was read out:

that you did feloniously kill and murder one Louisa Claydon, your wife, in a bedroom at … Portland Street at some time between 11 p.m. on Saturday, 6 July 1901 and 9.45 a.m. on Sunday, 7 July 1901.

Claydon said nothing in answer to the charge. Instead he stood in the dock smiling in a curious and content manner. He was remanded in custody for one week.

An initial inquest was held on the Monday after the crime before Borough Coroner, C. C. Becke. The formalities of identification of the remains and the details of the suspect in custody were reiterated before it was adjourned to the following week to allow the police to gather further evidence and witness information. The crime was big news in Northampton and the surrounding area, reporters clamouring to speak with anyone connected to either the family or the neighbourhood.

On Monday, 15 July, Alderman Cleaver, deputising for the Mayor, opened the committal proceedings. Kate Wareing was first to give evidence, deeply distressed by the situation and sobbing mournfully, she had to sit down so that she did not pass out, and was permitted to remain seated while giving her evidence. She told the packed courthouse that she had been sitting downstairs with her mother when Claydon had returned home around 11.15 p.m. on the night of Saturday, 6 July. He was, in her opinion, slightly the worse for drink; she could positively say this as she knew him well and lived in the same house as him. Continuing, she then told how she was in her bedroom at around 2.00 a.m. when she was awakened by her lamp being lit. It was Alex Claydon, demanding something to eat. Kate had told him to go away and shouted for her mother, but received no response. Claydon, she claimed, stood looking at her and demanded that she make him something to eat. Sternly, she told him to blow the candle out and to go back to bed. This he did, closing both bedroom doors as he went. She had then heard nothing until around 10.00 a.m. on the Sunday morning when she went into her mother's room to call her for breakfast. 'Everything was covered in blood!' she exclaimed. She continued to explain how Alex had been 'on the drink' for a fortnight and how the couple had argued over this fact and also that he refused to get work.

Claydon interrupted proceedings and said that what his daughter said was the truth, other than the fact that he wouldn't work. He claimed he couldn't find work. The clerk ordered him to silence and warned him not make a statement.

Susan Langley, the landlady of *The Engineer* public house, described the carnage she encountered on entering the bedroom after being alerted to the crime by Kate.

> *I found the deceased lying on the bed in a pool of blood, quite dead. There was a tassel off the edge of the quilt in her mouth. I tried to lift her head up, but it was stuck to the pillow by blood, and the pillow came up as well. There was a file on the bed.*

The movements of Alex Claydon prior to the crime were then provided. Isaac Finedon, the landlord of the *Old Globe*, told how Claydon had come to his hostelry on the Saturday night with no money. Finedon had refused to serve him because of this. He remained in the pub for around two hours, having found some friends to buy him drinks. He went out once but returned shortly after. Louisa Claydon had come into the pub at around 9.00 p.m. with washing and was given a glass of ale as a reward. While she was drinking the ale, Alex had gone up to her and whispered something in her ear, and in response to this she had turned away and given him no answer. She soon left the pub. Claydon had left the pub at about 11.00 p.m. Finedon had thought him to be perfectly sober. Claydon had been smiling continually throughout this evidence, and from the dock he responded to the statement, almost patronisingly, 'Why, Mr Finedon, your statement's wrong from beginning to end.'

Joseph Lack, a labourer from Kingsthorpe, then told the court how he had seen Claydon at *The Telegraph* public house in Moulton at 9.00 a.m. on the morning of Sunday, 7 July 1901. The men struck up a conversation about Lack's dog, before sitting down on a bench outside the pub, whereon Claydon had apparently told the unsuspecting labourer,

> *I feel 'dicky'. I have been on the booze this last fortnight. I've got something to tell you – a story. I went out last night and had a pint or two of beer. I left my wife in the bar and went into the parlour, and stayed until closing time, and went home. My wife was abed, asleep. I got into bed with her, and she said she should sooner have a serpent beside her than me. I lay down and went to sleep. Then I went down to my workshop and fetched my rasp. I hit her on the forehead, and stabbed her in the heart.*

Lack told the court how he hadn't believed the story but said that Claydon had then told him that he had a knife in his pocket and intended to do for himself. The men had then got up from the bench and walked some way before reaching the *Old Bluebell Inn*. Claydon had then said, 'That's the old place I've used many a time. I should like to go in there for the last time. You buy the drink, and I'll go to the police with you.' Once again Claydon denied a less-than-damning part of the evidence, stating, 'I never asked you to go to no constable. I've knowed where he lives for the last twenty years.'

Next to give evidence was Constable Bailey of the Northamptonshire County Police.

I met the prisoner at 5.45 a.m. on a side road near Buttocks Booth. He enquired the way to Moulton, but he went away in the direction of Boughton. At 9.45 a.m. he came with Lack to my station. He said, 'I didn't think you were stationed here, when I met you this morning. Did you think I was in a mizzy mozzy? I believe I have murdered my wife.' I cautioned him. He then unbuttoned his coat and showed me some bloodstains on the front of his shirt, and on the palms of his hands. He said 'That tells you a tale.' He made a statement 'Last night at 9.15, I met my wife in the Old Globe, on the Kettering Road. I asked if she was all right. She said, 'Are you?' and I said 'Yes'. I remained there till eleven, and then went home directly, and up to bed. I had no light. My wife was in bed. She called me a dirty dog, and said she would sooner have a serpent sleep with her than me. I said nothing and did nothing. I then went to sleep until 1.00 a.m. I believe I got up and went down to my shop and got my file; and I struck her on the head with it. I then went downstairs and had two eggs and bread and butter. I went back to bed and slept until a quarter to four. When I woke, I put my hands on my wife's body and found it was cold, I then got up and went for walk.

Again Claydon was asked if there was anything he would like to ask the officer, and again he made an unnecessary point, remarking that he felt that no statement should have been obtained from him in the state he was at the time of reporting the incident.

The police continued to give evidence. Sub-Inspector Allen told the court;

Going upstairs into the front bedroom, I saw the deceased on a bed, which stood just in front of the door. She was lying on her right side, dead. The bed clothes were all saturated with blood, and the wall beside her was besmeared with blood. I lifted her up and examined her. On the left side of her head, near the temple, was a large scalp wound, two inches long and very deep. On the left side of the neck was a hole, apparently from a stab, two inches below the left ear; and another just under the left breast, and over the heart, all of which appeared to have been done by the end of the file which had blood, flesh and hair on it. The left arm, which was raised from the body in an attitude of defence, was covered with bruises, extending from the wrist to the shoulder, and there were several stabs near the elbow, the bone of which appeared to be broken. Her fingers were clenched, and between them I found several short hairs which corresponded with the hair on the prisoner's head. I took possession of them. There did not appear to have been a struggle, as the bed clothes were in order, and the furniture was not disarranged. The hair on the file corresponded with that on the head of the deceased.

Alex Claydon was then committed for trial at the November Assizes in Northampton.

On Thursday, 23 November 1901 the case began before Sir John Charles Bigham, who appointed Ryland Adkins to defend the accused, while Lacey Smith offered the case for the prosecution. The case was clear-cut, all the evidence, including that of Alex Claydon indicating that he had committed wilful murder. Ryland Adkins. a master barrister of the circuit, was in no doubt of his client's guilt. However, he offered insanity as a possible defence for the crime. Like a theatrical performer with a fully attentive audience who were transfixed by his every word, he told the court,

The Claydon family are drenched with insanity, and burdened with a curse only one little bit less dreadful than that of drink. Bred of lunatics and tainted with drink, at the time of the murder, he was not earning money and was giving his time to self-indulgence. Can you imagine the man sleeping with the woman after he had murdered her? The violence he used was wholly unnecessary where one blow was sufficient to cause death.

It was a heartfelt and thoroughly sensible conclusion to draw. However, it was not one which the presiding Judge felt logical, and he was to instruct the jury as such. In summing up all the evidence for the jury, Mr Justice Bigham informed them,

> *There is not the ghost of evidence that there was anything of the nature of a quarrel, and the prisoner has not even suggested it. When a man deliberately goes away to fetch an instrument with which he then kills his wife, that is NOT manslaughter. This is a case of murder, and the only real question is whether, when he did the act, he knew he was doing wrong. The fact that he was drunk is no excuse for crime. I need not tell you of the consequences which might follow from your verdict. That is nothing to do with you.*

After such a defined summing-up, there was never any doubt what the jury's verdict would be; guilty of murder. The packed courtroom seemed, as one, to give a sigh of relief that the right and proper verdict had been found. The Judge had the black cap placed on his head as the court fell into a deathly silence. Looking sternly at Claydon, Mr Justice Bigham said,

> *Claydon, you have been found guilty, on evidence which I think to be irresistible, of the murder of your wife. It was a cruel, heartless murder. I may say this: that I daresay it would not have happened if you had not given way to this horrible vice of drunkenness, but the fact that you gave way to that vice, and that has undoubtedly led you to commit the crime, affords, in my eyes, no extenuation. It remains the same wicked and cruel murder. I shall say no more except this: that I advise you to prepare yourself for the end, which I believe, is very near. The sentence upon you is that you be taken hence to the place of execution and that you be there hanged by the neck until you be dead, and that your body be buried within the precincts of the prison in which you were last confined.*

Vicious killer Alex Claydon was hanged by the neck at 8.00 a.m. on Friday, 13 December 1901 at Northampton County prison by Billington.

Chapter 11

Much Too Young
1904

All children are beautiful miracles of life.
Why then do they commit murder at such a tender age?

George Burrows was a widower who lived in Ivy Road, Northampton. A hard-working man, he had contended with some of the most atrocious circumstances life could throw at anyone. The sad loss of his wife had hit him hard, but with a supportive family of six children, George managed to survive and raise what seemed to the outside world a caring and loving family. Five of his six children: Beatrice, aged 18; Elsie, aged 11; Thomas, aged 10; George junior, aged 15; and Harry, aged 8, all lived at home with him.

Unknown to this caring man and father, there were some problems that existed between the children and particularly with George junior. The fifteen-year-old had a truly sadistic streak in him, effectively born out of the loss of his mother and him seeking validation from his father and respect from the rest of the family. Thomas suffered greatly as a victim of his older brother's bullying and abuse. Regularly, George would get him by himself and then beat him, call him names and generally humiliate him in what now seems an organised and calculated manner. The attacks were consistent in their delivery process, inasmuch as neither the children's father nor Beatrice was ever about to witness them. Worse still, the beatings were underpinned with threats of worse to come if ever the father or Beatrice got to know or hear of them. It has to be said that there was no material reward or benefit gained by George junior when he carried out these blatant acts of thuggery and torture. Therefore it must have been through personal or sexual gratification that he delivered them.

On the night of Wednesday, 17 February 1904, at around 8.20 p.m. George senior left his house for a few minutes on an errand. He left behind Beatrice and George junior, who were both quietly sitting downstairs. Elsie, Thomas and Harry, meanwhile, were all upstairs and in their beds. Beatrice had an appointment and had to go out too, leaving the premises about ten minutes after her father at 8.30 p.m. This left George alone downstairs. The children upstairs, Thomas, Harry and Elsie, heard Beatrice leave the house. Thomas at once went into a self-preservation mode. Not wanting to have to suffer the sadistic tendencies of George junior, on hearing Beatrice leave, the ten-year-old at once jumped out of his bed, moved stealthily to his bedroom door and locked it to prevent his brother from getting in. He could hear George coming upstairs, the steady sound of his footsteps on each step terrifying him.

(After the evening's events, he was asked why he had been scared enough to lock the door. It was then that the awful reality of the matter came to light. He said he locked himself in his bedroom because he thought George would come in and start hitting him, which he had done on more than occasion previously.)

He breathed a sigh of relief when he realised George had bypassed him and instead gone to see Elsie in her bedroom. Confusion reigned when, soon after, he heard his sister repeatedly cry out 'Stop it, our George!' Little could the child have known what atrocities were taking place only a few feet from his own bedroom and ultimately his place of safety. A few moments later, George junior was banging around and making a lot of noise. He seemed, so far as Thomas could tell, to hurriedly leave the house, slamming the door behind him.

The young boy could tell that something wasn't right, but he was so frightened of his brother and what he might do to him that he stayed where he was for a few minutes, too terrified to move. It wasn't long before his emotions got the better of him and he burst into tears, though this was perhaps more out of relief because he could hear his father coming in.

Thomas unlocked his bedroom door and ran out to greet his father, who was surprised to see his son in such an awful emotional state. Checking on the welfare of his children, George senior moved from bedroom to bedroom, and was mortified to find Elsie lying on her bed, covered in blood and matter. The young girl's head had been almost completely smashed in by heavy blows from a blunt instrument. Thomas blurted out what he had heard through his bedroom door.

George senior must have been in complete turmoil on hearing what his son was saying and trying to accept that one of his own children had inflicted such an awful attack on a fellow sibling. Elsie was still breathing. George's immediate concern was for the welfare of his daughter. A doctor was summoned and did what he could to preserve life. However, the injuries were just too serious and complicated for Elsie to survive. She died at 10.15 p.m. without regaining consciousness, and therefore couldn't explain what had actually happened.

The police were called and it was quickly ascertained that the murder weapon was an axe which had been found nearby. Due to the bludgeoning of the skull it was clear that the injuries had been from the blunt end of the head of the axe as opposed to the blade. Whether this was by design or by the killer instinctively smashing the weapon down without caring which end makes contact with the skull was never ascertained. Clearly, bludgeoning would potentially inflict more structural damage, though the overall effect would be identical: serious injury.

George junior was soon in police custody and charged with the murder of his sister. He confessed to killing her. The subsequent trial was not filled with intrigue and legal argument between defence and prosecution barristers. It was a genuinely sombre affair which centred on questions surrounding the sanity of the accused boy. There was discussion about how 'fond' of Elsie George actually was. It was claimed that he regularly tended to her needs and cared for her, providing her with little gifts. Indeed, he had actually kissed her goodnight a few minutes before repeatedly bringing an axe down on her head. It was never fully discussed whether there was any kind of sexual 'fondness' displayed by George junior. The one witness who could have relayed this information was now dead. It has to be said that George did seem to have an unhealthy 'fondness' for Elsie, hence, perhaps, his sexual advances towards his sister were rebuffed that evening, resulting in her cries for him to stop it. The sexual rejection may well have caused him to react in such a barbaric manner and to destroy the object of his desires.

At the trial doctors discussed his mental state, and clearly there were many issues. For one thing he was described as constantly reading

Angel Lane police station, where George Burrows junior was taken and held.

what was referred to as 'sensational literature' and comics of 'criminal adventure' including such titles as *Buffalo Bill* and *Charlie Peace*. A psychiatrist who examined him, a Dr Harding of Northampton Berry Wood Asylum, said that in his professional opinion, George was suffering from 'homicidal mania – homicidal insanity'. This was as a direct result of the literature he read. The doctor confidently stated that he felt the mania was caused by the contents of such literature and therefore had caused George junior to kill his sister in such a dastardly manner.

The jury had little option but to return a verdict of not guilty by reason of insanity. The fifteen-year-old boy, George Scott Burrows, was then ordered to be detained at Her Majesty's pleasure. He remains the youngest person to be indicted for the charge of murder in Northampton.

While George Scott Burrows is the youngest person to be indicted on a charge of murder in the county, Arthur Pittam, at the age of just seven, is the youngest person to be brought before Judge and Jury in Northampton on a charge of manslaughter.

This sad tale took place on a Friday evening in 1897. Young Arthur, a spirited and often feisty child, arrived home filled with hunger. Entering the house he found his mother suckling his five-week-old sister, Sarah Ann. Arthur at once demanded the attention of his mother, asking her for food. The patient mother explained that she was unable to make him anything, after all could he not see she was otherwise engaged in feeding his baby sister. Without an ounce of malice, she told Arthur to help himself to some bread and butter which was on the kitchen table. In most situations, this would not be viewed as a precursor to a violent act or reaction.

However, to the highly charged and overactive mind of Arthur Pittam this was a lack of mother's interest and loss of validation. The simple fact that his mother did not jump up and immediately tend to his wishes sent young Arthur into an agitated and volatile state. Momentarily intent on hurting his mother, he picked up a butter knife, moved towards his seated mother and threw it at her. The weapon missed its target but struck the baby on a vulnerable spot on the top of her still-forming skull. The result was catastrophic; Sarah Ann cried uncontrollably for many hours, before she slipped into an unconscious state, and died two days later.

Just how a mother suckling a child deals with this scenario is beyond my comprehension. It must be difficult for any parent to have to deal with the fact that one of their own children possessed so much evil as to kill a sibling.

It is almost unheard of for a seven-year-old child to appear before any kind of court; at such a tender age, children are not deemed capable of malicious intent. One judicial test has always been to ascertain whether the child knows the difference between right and wrong. Even then it is open to debate that the surroundings of a courtroom can be a contributing factor to whether a child is mentally capable or prepared to withstand the serious workings of the environment. In this instance, the trial Judge, Mr Justice Pollock, had to formally discuss the legal position with the jury and the court itself.

The prisoner being only seven years of age, the inference of the law being that he could not suppose to be guilty of a crime because he was wanting in that wicked mind, which alone, could constitute a crime. There may be cases with defendants as young as this; there might be express malice which showed that he might be treated as another person should be. It would be a matter for the jury as to what the real act of this child was.

It was further stated by the defence counsel during the trial that 'the mental health of this family is terrible'. This potentially provided an insight as to why young Arthur reacted so badly to the situation. It did not, however, justify the reaction.

With this kind of statement being made, effectively, there was no case to answer. Yes, all agreed that it was known that Arthur had 'possibly' wanted to hurt his mother in a fit of temper, hence him throwing the knife. He had not, though, intended to murder or to kill anyone. It was a reckless and foolish act that would affect him for the rest of his life. The jury refuted the charge against him but gave strict provisos through the prosecuting barrister, Mr Ryland Adkins. They stated that they did not wish any punishment to be administered and that they would be very thankful if the boy (who would be taken away from his mother) could be cared for in a home for children who suffer such problems.

The likes of these two dreadful and harrowing cases continue to occur today. In the first instance, George Burrows junior was allegedly influenced by comic books. Today it might be put down to 'video nasties' or violent computer games. The second instance might currently be put down to Attention Deficit Hyperactivity Disorder.

Chapter 12

Polly, Put the Kettle on
1904

Kettering, one of the country's quiet market towns?
Was the famous nursery rhyme a ballad
about a wicked murder here?

It wasn't unusual for Sarah Ellen Smith of Northall Street, Kettering, to be out in the rear yard of her home. Without being too discriminatory, she was regarded locally as something of a nosey neighbour and therefore a good source of gossip. In the early evening of 27 July 1912, Sarah went out into her yard so that she could listen to another of the regular arguments which were taking place between the couple three doors along the street.

Smith had already ascertained that the residents of that property were unmarried. Northampton-born Mary Jane (Polly) Pursglove, who was thirty-six, was living with thirty-year-old Isaac Edward (Sukie) Sewell, who hailed from nearby Pytchley. It was somewhat frowned on that the man was six years younger than her. The couple's screaming matches were another common conversation piece in the neighbourhood. Sarah Smith rather enjoyed being able to listen to every word of the couple's arguments without fear of being seen; she lived two cottages down from the bothersome couple and was therefore well protected from view in her own yard.

Polly had been married to a soldier. However, the relationship had floundered and the couple split up after six years. For some reason she then took the surname Pittam and told people her husband had died in the war. Moving over to Kettering she took up with a railway-engine driver called Bell, with whom she lived in Carrington Street, Kettering, for a number of years. The family (minus Bell) had moved into Northall Street only five weeks earlier. Polly had a thirteen-year-old son who was in a reformatory, and had two daughters living with her, named Elizabeth Mary and Gladys.

From what Sarah Smith was able to glean from the comfort of her own back yard, Sewell was utterly jealous of Polly's ex-partner, Mr Bell, whom he had convinced himself Polly was still seeing. Circumstantial evidence does seem to exist which tends to support his suspicions. The Wednesday before the current argument, she had overheard Sewell say to Pursglove, 'If you go to Bell's any more I will be the death of you. If I catch him around here, I'll bloody well do for you!' his irate voice had bellowed. Now, during this latest confrontation, it was an extremely angry and agitated-sounding Polly who screamed at her partner, 'If you don't leave this roof, I shall. I am not going to have my life threatened. This is not the first time you said it!' Sewell had responded in a more reasoned and calm fashion, simply saying, 'All right, Polly.'

Sarah Smith strained to hear more of the quarrel, but the shouting had stopped. The couple, she thought, had closed the back door; either that or Elizabeth Mary Pursglove, Polly's eighteen-year-old daughter, had possibly intervened and calmed things down between the couple.

At around 6.00 p.m., Elizabeth left the house by the front door, and Sarah Smith made sure she was there to greet the young woman. Sarah wasn't too shy to ask the young woman if everything was now all right after the earlier argument. Elizabeth told her that her mum and Sukie had now calmed down, the confrontation was over and both were now quite happily shelling peas as though nothing had happened. Rather disappointed that there was nothing else she could actively gossip about to her peers, Sarah bid Elizabeth goodnight and returned indoors to continue with her domestic chores.

It wasn't long before she was interrupted by someone knocking at the front door of her home. Going out to see who it was, Sarah was greeted by six-year-old Gladys Pursglove, Polly's youngest. The child was barefoot and crying, 'Our Ted won't let me in!', Ted being Isaac Edward Sewell.

Sewell was a shoe repairer by trade and had taken her shoes from her with genuine intent to repair them. He had then told her to get out of the house and closed and locked the door behind her. A few minutes later, he too had left the house, again closing and locking the door behind him, thus leaving Gladys locked out. 'Where's your mother?'

asked Sarah Smith. 'Mama's in bed,' the young girl replied. 'Well, we will just have to wake her, won't we?' responded Smith comfortingly.

They both went first to Polly's front door and rapped on it several times. A few neighbours came out to see what all the fuss was about. Receiving no reply, they went round to the back, but again the door was locked and still there was no response. Smith then returned to the front of the house, and to get Gladys inside, lifted her through a front-room window which she had been able to force open. With the commotion over, everyone made their way back to their homes. Front doors had hardly been closed before a piercing scream filled the air. It was Gladys Pursglove. 'Mama's all over with blood!' she exclaimed. Sarah Smith was first in through the back door of the house, and ran up the stairs to the master bedroom, where she knew Polly slept. There lying on the bed was the woman, saturated in blood. There was so much of it about the body and the bed that it was difficult to identify just what it was she was looking at. Mrs Smith fainted. She was duly carried home by other neighbours, and Gladys was taken with her.

Another neighbour made his way upstairs and surveyed the scene. Polly Pursglove's throat had been cut so deeply that she had almost been decapitated. The blood that had spurted from the severed carotid artery had virtually drained the head and neck clean of any blood. The dead woman's clothes, bed linen, mattress and the surrounding bedroom floor were saturated with blood, some of which had started to congeal. It was a ghastly sight which sickened all who saw it. Turning away, the neighbour ran down the stairs and shouted to the gathered crowd outside the house, 'For God's sake, fetch the police.'

Back in her own house, Sarah Smith had little Gladys put to bed with a member of her own family in an attempt to calm things down. She sent one of her other children round to Wadcroft to bring Polly's mother, Mrs Catherine Heydon, to the house immediately.

Sergeant George Marsh was one of the first police officers at the scene. He was later to recall the carnage as 'among the most horrible death scenes he had ever encountered.' The officer knew of some of the issues surrounding the couple, because rumours had circulated about the constant arguments. Arriving in Northall Street, he met with neighbours who were all too keen to fill him in with all the gory details of what had happened. Marsh, forever the professional, maintained a calm manner during his initial inquiries. At the murder scene his sharp eyes noticed, just inside the doorway of the bedroom, Isaac Sewell's cap, and close to this was a bloodstained knife with hair still attached to the blade.

A doctor was called to the scene. Dr Lee certified life extinct and noted, along with Dr Gillispie, how the deceased was fully dressed, lying on her right side with the left hand uppermost. There was a large clot of blood on the floor as well as blood on the bed and bedding. He turned the dead woman over onto her back and saw two wounds in her neck, an upper and a lower wound. The lower wound was from the right side to the left and was not the fatal cut. This had still been severe enough to separate the thyroid cartilage and the vocal chords. The upper wound was, in the doctor's opinion, the fatal one. This started at the windpipe and went behind the right ear near to the back of the neck. It was deep enough to reach the base of the tongue, ripping open the jugular vein and slicing open muscle tissue. A piece of one of the small bones in the neck had been splintered by the force of the incision. There was little or no sign of any kind of struggle.

Elsewhere, away from the murder scene, Edward Sewell had in fact been arrested at around 9.30 p.m. initially for being drunk and disorderly. He had arrived in the passage of the home of Polly's mother, Catherine Heydon, that evening. A lodger at her Wadcroft home, Joseph Saddington, who himself had earlier been drinking with Sewell in the *Old White Horse*, was surprised to see him come through the back door of 17 Wadcroft and collapse in a drunken heap on the floor. Saddington, at the request of Catherine Heydon, removed Sewell from the house and put him out into the street, where he was arrested by the police shortly after. A description of the man wanted for the murder of Polly Pursglove had been disseminated soon after the discovery of the body. Kettering was then a small town with good communication, so Constable Taylor instantly recognised Sewell as the man wanted for the murder and picked him up from the gutter to confront him. On getting him to his feet, Sewell verbally abused him, and was arrested for being drunk and disorderly and taken directly to Kettering Police Station. Sergeant Marsh saw the wanted man in the custody of Constable Taylor and he too returned to the police station.

Taking the prisoner from Constable Taylor, Marsh escorted the drunken and abusive Sewell to his cell in the company of Inspector

Dunn. George Marsh knew instinctively he had his man. The prisoner was rambling insensibly, and, without any provocation or influence from the police officers, proffered; 'I have murdered a girl tonight. I cut her bloody head off. You need not trouble, I will hang.'

It was the following morning before he was sober enough to be interviewed and ultimately charged with murder. Further witnesses were spoken to and it was ascertained that after he had murdered Polly Pursglove he went to the *Three Cocks* public house further along Northall Street, arriving there around 7.30 p.m. There he drank two penny's worth of whisky before bidding landlord William Coleman goodnight and leaving. From there he went to the *Old White Horse* public house and drank a beer with Joseph Saddington. Leaving that pub after about ten minutes, Sewell wandered alone along Silver Street and down Market Street, where he met another acquaintance, Leonard Essam. It was now about 8.30 p.m. and he tried to persuade Essam to go drinking with him. Essam walked back to the *Old White Horse* with him, where they were refused a drink and asked to leave. Leonard Essam, realising his friend was too drunk to look after himself, offered to walk him to his home. Sewell refused to allow him do this, stating, 'No, you won't see me down Northall Street any more. You won't see me any more after tonight. You don't know what I know. You won't see me anymore.' Essam told him not to be foolish and so left him. From there Sewell had made his way to Catherine Heydon's home in Wadcroft, where he was arrested.

In his formal statement to the police, Sewell said;

> *I know I done it. I done it about seven o'clock , we were both lying on the bed and I went downstairs and fetched my knife. She was nearly asleep. She never called out. I went out and got drunk. It is all through her going to Bell's.*

Judicial matters moved reasonably swiftly and a few days later at the coroner's inquest the jury were told that the crime was committed without provocation and therefore the only verdict they could return was one of wilful murder against Sewell. Three minutes later the jury returned a guilty of murder verdict.

A special sitting of the Kettering Police Court was held on Tuesday, 8 August 1912 before magistrates J. A. Gotch (Chairman), Wallace Willows, J. T. Stockburn, A. Mackay, and C. Barlow. Sewell did not

ALLEGED MURDER.

Aug-9-1912

THE KETTERING CHARGE.

Committed for Trial.

At a special sitting of Kettering Police Court, which was held on Tuesday, Isaac Edward Sewell, a shoehand of Kettering, was charged on remand with the wilful murder of Mary Jane Pursglove, a woman with whom he lived in Northall-street, on July 27th:—The magistrates present were J. A. Gotch, Esq. (chairman), Wallace Willows, J. T. Stockburn, A. Mackay, and C. Barlow, Esqs.

The prisoner, who badly wanted shaving, still appeared not to realise the perilous position in which he stands, and followed the hearing of the evidence with not too close attention. After he had been committed, and on leaving the dock prisoner winked at two acquaintances who were in the body of the crowded Court.

Mr. W. R. Lay, prosecuted on behalf of the Director of Public Prosecutions, and Mr. Evan Barlow (Leicester) defended.

At the outset Mr. Lay apologised to the Court for being late. He outlined the case and gave practically the same facts as appeared in our columns last week. In conclusion he said the case was a simple one of wilful murder. Jealousy seemed to be the motive which prompted the crime, but jealousy was no excuse for murder.

The first witness called was Elizabeth Mary Pursglove, a single woman, living at 17, Wadcroft. She said Mary Jane Pursglove, the murdered woman, was her mother. For about five weeks before July 27th her mother, herself, and a younger sister, named Gladys, lived at 76, Northall-street. The prisoner had been living with the family and cohabiting with the dead woman. During the five weeks they had lived in Northall-street there had been a few quarrels, and prisoner accused the dead woman of going with a man named Bell. On the Wednesday previous to the murder there was a quarrel and the prisoner said "If you go to Bell's any more I will be the death of you." On the Saturday afternoon of the murder witness, her little sister and Sewell, were together. Her mother came home shortly after four o'clock. About an hour later accused and her mother had a quarrel and the woman said "If you don't leave this roof I shall, as I am not going to have my life threatened. This is not the first time you said it." Accused said "Alright Polly." Both then became quiet, and witness left

the house about six o'clock, both her mother and Sewell being then on good terms. Witness last saw a knife (produced) in a drawer in the house on Saturday afternoon about three o'clock. Accused was a rivetter.

Sarah Ellen Smith, wife of Frederick Smith, an ironstone labourer, said she lived at 79, Northall-street. There are two cottages between witness's house and that in which Mrs. Pursglove lived. Witness only heard a few words between Sewell and the dead woman the week previous to the murder. On the 27th July she heard the woman tell Sewell she would not allow him to stay under her roof another night. About eight o'clock on the night of the murder the little daughter of the deceased woman, named Gladys, went to witness and in consequence of what she told her she went to Mrs. Pursglove's house and found both doors locked. She opened the front downstairs window and put the child through into the room. Witness went back home, but only just got to her house when she heard a scream, and witness went back. The little girl unlocked the back door and witness went into the house and then upstairs. She saw the deceased lying on the bed fully dressed, and after striking a light found Mrs. Pursglove had had her throat cut and appeared to be dead. Witness sent for the police, and Sergt. Marsh shortly afterwards arrived.

P.S. Marsh said he was called to the deceased's house on the night of the murder. He found the poor woman on a bed in the back bedroom, quite dead. Witness made a search of the room and found the knife (produced) covered with blood and with hair adhering to it. On the same side of the bed about a foot from the knife he found the cap produced. Both a doctor and Inspector Dunn were sent for. Afterwards, about 9.50, he saw the accused being taken to the Police Station by P.C. Taylor. Witness and Inspector Dunn took the man to the cells. He was in a very drunken condition. He said "I have murdered a girl to-night. I cut her —— head off. You need not trouble. I know I shall hang." At the time he made that statement nothing had been said to him about the murder which had taken place. At the police station the key of the front door was found in the pocket of prisoner's clothes. There did not appear to be any signs of a struggle.

Dr. Lee was called on the night of the tragedy to the house of the woman Pursglove. He found her dead, lying on the bed fully dressed. He thought she had been dead about two hours. She was lying on her right side with the left hand uppermost. There was a large clot of blood on the floor as well as on the bed and bedding. Witness turned the woman on to her back and saw two wounds on the neck. There was an upper and lower wound. The lower wound extended from the right side to the left, severing the windpipe and arteries. The wound was a clean cut and had apparently been made by one cut. This wound would not probably have caused death. The upper wound was longer and much deeper, commencing about the middle of the wind pipe passing below the right ear to the back of the neck. The edges of the wound were irregular and jagged and appeared to have been made by more than one effort. This wound divided the principal structors, all the arteries and muscles being severed. A piece of one of the small bones of the neck was splintered, indicating considerable violence. The wounds could not have been self-inflicted and could have been done with such a knife as the one (produced). Death would rapidly follow. Witness performed a post-mortem examination. Deceased was a perfectly healthy woman, and there was nothing to account for death beyond the wounds in the neck.

Dr. Gilispie, assistant to Dr. Allison, said in company with Dr. Lee, he saw the dead woman, and corroborated the evidence he had given.

Wm. Coleman, landlord of the "Three Cocks," Kettering, said the accused went

into his house about 7.30 o'clock. He came from the direction of Northall. He asked for 2d. whisky. He appeared perfectly sober and seemed in a great hurry. He drank up his whisky and went off.

Catherine Heydon, mother of the deceased, living at 17, Wadcroft, said she saw her daughter on the Saturday morning of the murder. The same evening she saw the accused. He was lying down in her passage very drunk. Mr. Saddington picked accused up and put him into the street. About eight o'clock she saw prisoner near the Old White Horse. He said, "I want to speak to you." Witness said, "I have not got time. Tell dad (meaning Mr. Saddington), and he will tell me when he comes home." Prisoner then went into the Old White Horse public-house.

Joseph Saddington, a blacksmith, living at 17, Wadcroft, said the last witness was his housekeeper. On the Saturday evening of the murder witness was in the Old White Horse, and while there accused came into the public-house. He appeared to be quite sober. Witness asked him to drink, which he did, and then he (prisoner) paid for another one. Prisoner said, "I will have another drink and then go along the street. I will see you later." He was in the public house about ten minutes altogether. Later in the evening he saw accused at home. He came in at the back door and threw himself on the floor in a drunken condition. Witness then put the prisoner outside, and he was arrested by a policeman.

Leonard Essam, living at 22, Wood-street, Kettering, a shoe operator, said he knew the prisoner well. About 8.30 on the Saturday evening in question he saw the accused at the bottom of Market-street the worse for drink. Witness accompanied him along the street, and when they got to the Old White Horse they went in for a drink, but were refused by the landlord. Witness asked to take accused home, and he said, "No, you won't see me down Northall any more." Witness said, "Don't talk silly." Accused said, "You won't see me any more after to-night." Witness asked him why; was he going abroad? Prisoner said, "You don't know what I know." On parting at the top of Wadcroft prisoner kissed him and said "Good-bye; you won't see me any more." (Prisoner was noticed to smile).

P.C. Taylor said he was on duty in Wadcroft on the night of the murder, when he saw the prisoner lying down in the street very drunk. Witness assisted the man to his feet and brought him to the Police Station, in consequence of his description corresponding with that of the man who was wanted for the crime

Inspector Dunn, in giving evidence, said that on the back of the apron the woman was wearing there were several finger prints in blood. In the fire grate in the living room of the house he found some papers with fresh blood upon them. On the Sunday morning at the Kettering Police Station, prisoner was charged with the wilful murder of the woman Pursglove. Prisoner said, "I know I did it. I did it about seven o'clock. We were both lying on the bed, and I went downstairs and fetched a knife. She was nearly asleep. She never called out. I went out and got drunk. It is all through her going to Bell's."

The charge having been read over to the accused, he replied, in a firm voice, "I plead not guilty."

Accused was committed to take his trial at the next Assizes to be held in October.

THE CENOTAPH.

The Kettering cenotaph, in front of the Library, has lost its beauty; it is dirty and ill-cared for! The flowers placed there by bereaved parents are allowed to remain until they have long passed the withering stage, and disused jam jars, now empty, which once contained floral tributes, are about the base in disorder. This cenotaph has served its purpose, and should be taken down, and one worthy of the town erected as a reminder to the future generations of Kettering's part in the cause of right and freedom against might and Prussianism.

K.L. OCT.25TH 1912

NORTHAMPTON ASSIZES

ISAAC SEWELL. FOUND GUILTY BUT INSANE ORDERED TO BE CONFINED IN A CRIMINAL LUNATIC ASYLUM; DURING HIS MAJESTY'S PLEASURE

HOW KETTERING WON THE WAR.

The Kettering Remount Depot has long finished its usefulness, and has closed down. But how long would it have provided employment for high salaried officials had not pressure been brought upon the Government to practice what it preaches when it takes for its text "Economy?" Yesterday the component parts of the depot came under the hammer, and the public had the first chance of seeing what they had paid for. But little did the taxpayers realise that this war would not have been won had not the Kettering Remount Depot had five dog carts and a buggy, eight sets of silver and brass-mounted single harness, and the usual equipment of a gentleman's stable.

* * *

Newspaper coverage of the Kettering murder.

seem to realise the perilous position he was facing with the charges being preferred against him. The hearing heard a brief outline of the case and Sewell was committed to trial at Crown Court at the next Northampton Assizes. Quite incredibly, on leaving the dock, Sewell winked at two acquaintances he clearly recognised in the body of the crowded court.

The trial of Isaac Edward Sewell formally opened at Northampton Assizes on 18 October 1912. Sewell, wearing a dark-coloured suit with no collar, was a sullen and lonely figure. Throughout the trial, he kept his hands in his pockets and now struggled to make eye contact with anyone in the court, preferring instead to gaze at the ground in front of him. Sarah Smith told how, earlier on the day of the murder, Mrs Heydon had told her that Sewell had threatened to 'put Polly's lights out before the day was out'. In fact Polly had told her mother, 'Mother, I am between life and death.'

Medical evidence confirmed that Sewell was not insane at the time of the murder, nor did he suffer any form of mental illness. In an attempt to depict a rather different image, Sewell's two brothers told the court that they had an imbecile brother who was twenty-four years old and that they had two uncles who had committed suicide in the last couple of years. They further added that, in May 1908, Isaac had suffered a cycling accident in which he had fractured his jaw and, they believed, his skull. To support this they said he had been absent from his work for a month suffering from concussion. He had often complained of headaches and was often depressed and moody. He had in fact expressed a feeling that he wanted to die! He had on several occasions tried to slash his wrists with a razor and had to be restrained.

Another witness, a work colleague, explained that Sewell suffered from headaches and had at times been too ill to work. The day before the murder he had complained of feeling ill with bad headaches. It was also ascertained that on the Saturday before the murder, he had sharpened his knife to carry out repairs to Gladys's shoes.

In his summing-up the newly appointed judge, Mr Justice Scrutton, advised the jury that it was their role to consider whether or not it was possible for someone to commit a crime while he was temporarily insane, and then to recover his sanity soon afterwards. He pointed out that doctors and lawyers had disagreed on this point throughout the trial. While a person might be subject to an uncontrollable impulse, the legal definition of insanity was that if he knew what he was doing was wrong, then he was guilty, in spite of that uncontrollable impulse. The death sentence was there to make others think twice about giving in to such impulses.

The jury deliberated for forty-five minutes. On their return to the courtroom the spokesperson for the jury was asked, 'Is the prisoner guilty of intentionally killing Mary Jane Pursglove?' He replied, 'Yes.'

'Was he insane at the time he did so?' 'Yes,' came the reply, to the surprise and shock of all those gathered in the court. The judge sentenced immediately: 'It is the sentence of this court that the prisoner be detained in a lunatic asylum until His Majesty's pleasure be known.' So Isaac Sewell made the unexpected journey from the court to a lunatic asylum for the rest of his life.

There is a suggestion that the children's rhyme 'Polly, Put the Kettle on' refers to the facts surrounding this most awful crime. There can be no doubting there is much to support the suggestion!

Chapter 13

The Case of the Drunken Doctors 1924

*Doctors are meant to be paragons of virtue
charged with saving lives.
Not so this doctor, a reckless killer.*

It was approaching 8.30 p.m. on Whit Monday 1924, a clear and dry evening when 26-year-old John Rowlatt Corner, from Billesden in Leicestershire, was driving his motorcycle and sidecar combination carrying his fiancée, Sarah Lucy Harris. The young lovers were returning to Leicester after spending the bank holiday weekend at a secluded farmhouse in south Northamptonshire.

Corner was an experienced motorcyclist, having owned his own machine for three years with no accidents or injuries to talk of. As the couple drove along the quiet, tree-lined country road they undoubtedly felt quietly content that they were almost home after a weekend when they had relaxed and enjoyed time in each other's company away from the routine environment of work and everyday life.

Turning a bend in the road just passed Kelmarsh Hall, the couple saw a car about 200 yards ahead of them. John saw it straight away and was a little concerned as it was headed directly at them on the wrong side of the road. Slowing the motorcycle down to a crawl, he raised his hand in an attempt to catch the driver's attention. There was no response, and the approaching vehicle continued to speed towards them. By now both John and Sarah were getting anxious. Sarah was frantically waving both her arms in the air, while John sounded the motorcycle's horn. This too went apparently unnoticed. Gently pulling back the throttle to try to accelerate the motorcycle off the road, Corner swerved onto the edge of the nearside grass verge in a desperate attempt to avoid a collision. The car still raced towards them on the wrong side of the road. John Corner did what he could to take evasive action, but it was too late. The motorcycle and sidecar were struck side-on, throwing the machine, rider and sidecar occupant into the air, before it landed and rolled into the grass edge. Both rider and passenger were flung from the machine like rag dolls, Corner landing on the grass verge and Sarah on the road. Unfortunately for Corner the motorcycle landed on top of him, trapping him under the weight of its twisted frame. Still conscious, he hoped and expected to see the car driver emerge from the other crash vehicle and come to their assistance. The car continued on its way and disappeared round the bend. In agony, he cried out as there was a searing pain in his leg. He screamed and begged for assistance, but his cries went unheard and disappeared into the night air. Sarah Harris lay unconscious, partly on the road and partly on the grass verge.

As the darkness of the night closed in, John Corner could muster no more energy to cry for help, and he too collapsed into an unconscious state. The couple lay there for fully an hour before help arrived. An ambulance was summoned and arrived about twenty minutes later. Quickly the officer surveyed and assessed the injuries. Sarah Harris, despite being in the sidecar, which was hardly well protected, had received minimal injuries, a few cuts and bruises and nothing more. Corner was in a far worse state. He was taken to Northampton hospital, where his injuries were examined and detailed as a six- to seven-inch laceration on the front thigh and a two-inch cut to the rear thigh on his right leg; compound fractures of both bones in the same leg, with the lower part of the principal bone protruding some four inches to the front; severe cuts and lacerations to the lower lip and chin; two teeth missing, and one piece of lower jaw with teeth attached was hanging by the gum.

He was lucky to be alive. The examining doctors immediately carried out emergency surgery, plating the fractured bones and temporarily rebuilding his face. Despite the very best efforts of the medical team and due primarily to the delay in getting him to the hospital, the right leg had to be amputated as gangrene had set in. Some four days after the accident, John Corner died as a result of the injuries he had sustained in it.

The police made frantic efforts to trace the mysterious car and its driver. A full description was disseminated to the local press asking anyone with any information to come forward. A number of people did and eventually the car was traced to its owner, Dr Alexander John Douglas Cameron. He denied all involvement in any accident and effectively lied to save his own skin. A full inspection of the vehicle took place. Pieces of car running-board found at the scene of the crash were confirmed as coming from Cameron's car. Paint found on the motorcycle matched the colour and type of that on Cameron's car. The evidence was pretty conclusive. The doctor was arrested and questioned by the police.

In his statement he claimed that he was unaware of being in any incident or accident. He could clearly remember the motorcycle and sidecar running off the road near Kelmarsh but it was they, he suggested, who were on the wrong side of the road, not him! The police asked why he had not stopped when he saw the motorcycle run off the road, but he refused to answer. This was followed by a question about how his car had suffered damage that matched the collision damage on the motorcycle, and how he had failed to notice the obvious 'crash noise' caused by a collision. Again the doctor remained silent. He offered not one explanation for any of these issues. He displayed no remorse and showed no sympathy for the dead man or his family and friends, continuing to maintain his web of lies.

It later transpired that travelling with Cameron that evening was a Dr Duthie. Both men had been out to a cricket match. Duthie, when questioned, stated that they had been drinking for a number of hours, claiming that each of them had about five whisky-and-sodas. When this evidence was put to Cameron, he simply stated that he wasn't drunk.

Perhaps realising the gravity of the situation he was in, Duthie spoke openly about the journey that evening. He explained that Cameron was driving the car and as they passed Brixworth a charabanc had collided with their vehicle, causing damage to the vehicle's running-boards. The charabanc failed to stop so the doctors continued on their way. Shortly after this he had been involved in the motorcycle sidecar incident at Kelmarsh but had felt no tremor as a result of this. Shortly after passing through Kelmarsh the steering had become difficult and the front tyre had become soft. However, not wanting to stop to pump air into it, they had continued on their way to Northampton. On arrival at the opera house both men noticed that the complete rubber tyre was absent from the steel wheel rim. Somewhat dismissively, Cameron requested that a doorman either fix it or change the wheel for him while he watched the opera.

Cameron, he said, had not reported the motorcycle incident to the police as he was not aware that he had been involved in an accident, and he had not seen any newspapers for two or three days.

Both vehicles were examined by a London-based consultant motor engineer, Herbert William Bambar, who confirmed that paint from the motorcycle was evident on Cameron's car. This had been there as a result of the collision. The engineer further confirmed that scratches and dents on both vehicles matched the impact point on the road and metals respectively. He suggested that the underside of the cycle handlebar had run along the top of the wing, and that other damage was consistent rather with having been struck by the hub of another vehicle than by a motorcycle, on which he found nothing likely to cause the damage.

With respect to the motorcycle he said that the brakes were defective and the steering gear out of order. More incredibly, he declared that the footboard could have been ripped off the car without the driver actually knowing it had happened.

A special hearing was held at Northampton Assizes on Monday, 20 October 1924. Such was the interest in the case that special viewing tickets had to be issued to spectators. Court Commissioner Mr T. Hollis Walker explained the basis of the case to the jury, who were forced to endure four hours of conflicting evidence and written statements from all parties. The Crown, ably led by Sir Henry Maddocks KC, explained in some detail how two further witnesses had been forced off the road by Cameron's reckless driving that evening. Furthermore, other witnesses testified that they had seen the vehicle being driven in a dangerous manner and erratically through a number of towns and villages. Great emphasis was placed by the Crown on Cameron's apparently careless attitude towards the safety of his car and its general poor condition. Doubts as to the doctor's integrity were forming in the minds of the jurors.

THE KELMARSH TRAGEDY.

Northampton Doctor Sentenced to Nine Months' Imprisonment.

PROLONGED HEARING.

STORY OF CHARABANC WHICH COULD NOT BE TRACED

After a hearing extending over two days, Dr. Alexander John Douglas Cameron, aged 36, of Northampton, was found guilty at Northampton Assizes of manslaughter, and sentenced to nine months' imprisonment in the second division. The fatality to which the charge was the sequel, occurred on Whit-Monday at Kelmarsh. A young man named John Rowlatt Corner, aged 26, of Billesdon, was driving a motor-cycle combination along the Market Harborough road, from Hannington, in the direction of Harboro'. He had as passenger a young lady, Miss Lucy Harris. Just past Kelmarsh Hall, a car from the opposite direction approached, according to the evidence for the prosecution, on the wrong side. A collision occurred, Mr. Corner sustaining a fractured leg. The car, which contained Dr. Cameron and another doctor, did not stop. For an hour the injured man laid beside the road before medical aid could be secured, and four days later he died. Cameron was committed to the Assizes by the Kettering Bench, and on the warrant of the Coroner conducting the inquest upon Mr. Corner. The hearing opened at 1.35 on Monday afternoon and was concluded on Wednesday evening. The court was packed, tickets having to be issued owing to the great demand for seats.

Newspaper coverage.

Defence Barrister, Sir Ryland Adkins KC, attempted to denounce all that the prosecution had offered as evidence. In a lengthy and impassioned speech he made it quite clear that there was no wilful intent on the doctor's behalf to injure or maim anyone, and furthermore no doctor worth his salt would fail to stop and save a human life! Much was made of Cameron's fine social character, but more damage was done by the fact that he openly admitted to drinking heavily on the day of the accident.

Finally, during his summing-up of the case, Mr Justice Walker spoke of the mysterious charabanc incident which Cameron claimed to have been the cause of the damage to his car. Much effort had been put into trying to locate this vehicle, but no trace of it was ever forthcoming. In fact other witnesses who saw Cameron's car on the road at Brixworth had not sighted a charabanc along the route in question. He damningly pointed out the obvious by stating that this vehicle probably never existed.

The jury left the courtroom to deliberate their verdict and returned some thirty-five minutes later, with a guilty of manslaughter verdict. Dr Cameron was jailed for nine months. Yet the question remains, was he guilty of murder or not? Surely it is clear that in his statement to the authorities he consistently lied, the charabanc incident being just one case in point. His refusal to co-operate with the police was not conducive to a fine, upstanding gentleman, as doctors were, and to a certain extent still are, deemed to be.

To give him the benefit of the doubt, perhaps he was simply too drunk to realise what had actually taken place that fateful evening. His professional life was thereafter in ruins and quite rightly so. Who after all would want to be treated by a doctor whose principles were clearly not about saving the lives of others, but more selfishly about saving his own life. The verdict of manslaughter perhaps warranted a longer term of incarceration, but it does seem as though the case was treated in a more serious manner, with an initial charge of murder being brought against the doctor. If only such breeches of the law were treated so seriously and strictly today. Nine months does, though, seem to me a paltry sentence for someone who deliberately overindulged in alcohol before driving a car and took the life of another.

Chapter 14

Fake Life, Fake Death
1930

*A cocktail for disaster: an amorous garter salesman,
a car and a travelling man on bonfire night, fireworks and
one of the country's most infamous murder cases.*

In a quiet corner of a Northamptonshire graveyard lie the remains of a poor soul who met a most ignominious end. The grave is situated within the boundaries of the Hardingstone village churchyard. The remains are of an unknown man who died in 1925, having been decapitated in the nearby Hunsbury railway tunnel. The man was believed to have been a vagrant taking a shortcut to an unknown destination that he never reached. So badly mutilated were the remains that those who saw the body could no more identify it as a human being than as the carcass of a pig.

Despite the desperate pleas of the local authorities, not a single soul came forward to claim the remains, so his anonymity was set to remain for ever. The funeral of the man took place on 4 June 1925 and the then vicar of Hardingstone, Archdeacon Kitchen, conducted the burial service, which was kept private. The reason for the privacy was a simple one. Some local parishioners were not happy about such remains being buried in their parish, and there had been some doubt locally whether it was morally correct to bury it in consecrated ground when its provenance was not known. Archdeacon Kitchen was adamant that it was morally correct to have the remains laid to rest locally. Hence the privacy was to prevent outsiders and some villagers from identifying the precise location of the grave and to prevent its desecration.

There is nothing significantly strange or unusual about having the grave of an unknown corpse in the peripheries of any parish church. Indeed, such instances are reasonably common up and down the

United Kingdom. However, the quaint Northamptonshire village of Hardingstone is unique inasmuch as it has two such graves! Within a few yards of the original 'unknown man' lies the marked grave of a second such corpse. This time the death was no accident but an act of premeditated murder.

Just five years after the original burial, a second sensation shocked the village and, this time, the entire nation. The genteel inhabitants of this tranquil village awoke one cold November morning in 1930 to find their privacy disturbed by dozens of journalists keen to report on this latest sensation. The majority of the village had not the slightest idea that murder had occurred within close proximity of many of their homes: a man had perished in a blazing car in Hardingstone Lane.

The Domesday Book lists 'Hardingstorp' or 'Hardingstorn', the village's present name being a derivative of these. In modern times it is best described as a 'dormitory' for those wanting access to Northampton or for the nearby M1 motorway. It will always retain its village status despite the fact that the urban district of Northampton is fast expanding and almost enveloping it within the town boundary.

In 1930 it consisted of Coldstream Lane, Back Lane and the High Street. Access to the main routes through the village was via High Street, which subsequently merged into Hardingstone Lane. The latter has changed beyond all recognition; a bus stop now stands on the site where one of Britain's most sensational murders took place. A stone wall blocks the original lane, and behind it runs the busy A45 (Nene Way) dual carriageway, making it a very different place from the remote area it was in 1930.

The majority of people who lived in the village in 1930 have long since moved, but still the Blazing Car murder is a regular point of discussion, mainly because so many questions remain unanswered. Locally, the village is renowned for its abundance of wells. At one time there were over two hundred in the village, the majority having been filled after the typhoid epidemic of 1874, when, with no piped water supply, the stagnant water in the wells became polluted.

As well as an abundance of wells, Hardingstone had three ponds, all with varied and chequered histories. 'Lily Ocean' was situated off Hardingstone Lane on its western side, and was home to a variety of newts, frogs and flowering weed, making it a firm favourite with the village children. The water from Lily Ocean filtered down into a lower pond known as 'The Basin' and from there into 'Green Pond', which was at the bottom of the present Port Lane. This particular pond found fame in the 1940s when the *News of the World* newspaper covered a somewhat sad story; Bill Battison, a lengthsman who could be regularly seen clearing Hardingstone's streets of rubbish, had his companion dog with him at all times. The animal was something of a contentious point in the village; promiscuous and with appalling sanitary habits, it was generally unpopular. Despite receiving various warnings from locals, Bill did little to control his dog, refusing to keep it on a leash. Without warning the dog went missing, and Bill Battison was distraught. Eventually the animal was found, tied in a sack and drowned in Green Pond. Nobody confessed to the killing and the anxious press tried to identify suspects, but the village refused to co-operate and the mystery continued. Even today, those who were present at the time refuse to discuss the matter, other than saying that it was a visitor to the village who had killed the dog!

The Basin, meanwhile, held a more fearsome reputation – it was believed to be bottomless! The tale was further enhanced when a fire broke out at the Old Saw Mill and the local fire brigade pumped water from the pond to extinguish the fire. Despite the high quantity of water used in the fire-fighting, the water level of the pond never dropped. Local folklore then gave rise to talk of subterranean caverns and a fearsome monster that lived in the Basin! Today the ponds have all but disappeared and the mysterious 'beast' of the Basin has long since been forgotten. The memory of a different kind of beast lives on today: a cowardly and callous murderer, his name is Alfred Arthur Rouse.

It was around two o'clock on the morning of 6 November 1930 when William Bailey and Alfred Thomas Brown were making their way home on foot to Hardingstone after a bonfire-night celebration at the Salon club in nearby Northampton. The night was clear and crisp and the air filled with woodsmoke as bonfires all over the district burnt out the last of their dying embers.

Turning off London Road and into Hardingstone Lane the men saw clearly ahead of them a raging fire. Stepping out and walking along the lane, they were both shocked by the sudden appearance of a man from a nearby hedgerow on the south side of the lane. The man, who was wearing a knee-length raincoat and carrying a small overnight bag, emerged from the hedge, dusted himself down and made his way along Hardingstone Lane towards London Road. Witness Alfred Brown told me many years later,

> *We were surprised to see what looked like a respectable man coming from a hedge. Bill and I looked at one another in a confused way, but didn't say anything out loud about it as we didn't want to get involved with the stranger.*

Instead they discussed what the fire ahead of them could be. The stranger heard this comment and intervened, 'I think someone has had a bonfire,' he said, before hurrying off. Brown and Bailey stopped and turned to watch the man, who from his actions appeared rather agitated. On reaching the junction with London Road he first turned right and walked a couple of steps before again stopping, and looking aimlessly in both directions along the main road. He then looked back down Hardingstone Lane.

Feeling it best to continue on their way, both men continued their journey home. Turning a slight bend in the road, they encountered a gruesome and shocking scene. There before them was a parked car, which was on fire. Flames crackled and spat high into the night sky, the foul smell of burning oil and rubber and plastic filling the air. The car was a baby Morris Minor saloon and was completely engulfed by fire. Neither man could get close to it due to the searing intensity of the heat. Both men ran towards Hardingstone to raise the alarm. Alf went to fetch the village constable, PC Bert Copping, and Bill returned home to get his father, Hedley Bailey, who was the parish constable. The hue and cry raised alerted other village folk who made their way to the scene.

The police officers took control of the situation and directed the gathered throng to form a human chain to a nearby pond. Buckets filled with water were then passed back and forth and thrown over the fire. Twelve minutes later the fire was out.

Steam rose from the twisted and buckled metal frame that was once a motor car. The body of the vehicle was completely destroyed, but the aluminium registration plates were intact – MU1468 – at least the police had something to go on, as the vehicle would be registered on the national vehicle database (now known as PNC). Bert Copping was the first to walk up to the wreck and peer inside. Initially there didn't appear to be anything of note inside the wreckage. He called out to the others that there seemed to be a black-coloured and badly burnt rugby ball on the driver's seat. Alf Brown approached and shone his torch into the remains of the car. He recalls the scene:

> *I went over to stand beside the car, it was still hot. I shone my torch inside and immediately lit up the rugby ball shaped object on the front seat. There was a terrible smell, not rubber, not oil or petrol, a sickly odour like badly burnt bacon. I moved the light of my torch*

Alf Brown, who saw Rouse close to the murder scene.

> *across the front seats and Bert told me to hold the light still. As I did we made out the shape of human body laid across the front two seats. It then dawned on each of us that the rugby ball object was a human head.*

Bert noted that the remains were lying face down, the left arm tucked beneath what was left of the torso. The right arm had been burnt off at the elbow. In what looked like a remarkably uncomfortable position, the left leg was doubled up beneath the body, whereas the right leg had almost completely been destroyed by fire, making its positioning difficult to assess. Hedley Bailey was sent to summon assistance from the Northampton police headquarters.

It was close to three o'clock when Inspector James Lawrence arrived in Hardingstone Lane. He discussed the situation with Bert Copping, and a decision was made that in all probability the carnage that remained was as a result of a tragic accident. No other vehicle was involved and at that time, and no suspicious circumstances were noted.

The first thought was that the unidentified driver had accidentally set light to the car while lighting a cigarette or cigar. The basis for this assessment stemmed from the fact that behind one of the front seats a petrol can was clearly visible.

The body was removed from the car and taken to the garage of the *Crown Inn* in Hardingstone, later being transferred to Northampton General Hospital. The wreckage was dragged from its final resting place onto the grass verge to allow vehicle access along the route. Checks on the registration plate of the vehicle were requested from Scotland Yard and the police left the scene for the night.

At about eight o'clock that morning, Arthur Ashford, an enterprising and aspiring young photographer, made his way to the scene and took several photographs of the wreckage, moving various bits of the vehicle to make his shots more complete. At the time no one was to realise that the actions of the photographer and the failure of the police to recognise it as a crime scene, and thus to protect it to preserve evidence, could have serious consequences for the further investigation of the case.

Later that day, Scotland Yard returned the information about the registered owner of the burnt-out vehicle. It belonged to Alfred Arthur Rouse, of Buxted Road, Friern Barnet, North London. Rouse had been a commercial traveller for a Leicester firm which manufactured garters and suspenders. Enquiries were made at his home address. His wife, Lilian, had last seen him about eight o'clock the previous evening, when he left the family home to make his way to Leicester on business. Mrs Rouse explained that her husband always travelled alone. As a result of this information she was informed of the tragic accident and told to expect the worst, as human remains had been found in the vehicle.

As momentum gathered, the police realised that there had been some sinister issues surrounding the blaze. Bert Copping spoke to Alf Brown and Bill Bailey and suddenly the encounter with the stranger in the raincoat took on a different slant. Who was he? Why was he there?

With the human remains so badly destroyed by fire a limited forensic check was made of the remains. A crease in the crotch of the trousers had protected the cloth from damage. It had been saturated in petrol. The common belief was that the remains were those of Alfred Arthur Rouse, but who would want to kill him, and why do so in such a grotesque manner?

The police spoke with the press and asked for anyone with any information to come forward, especially regarding the possible identity of the 'city gent' who had been witnessed close to the scene by Brown and Bailey. Unknown to the police at that time, the stranger had been given a lift to South Wales by a passing lorry. Worse still, the stranger was in fact also the killer. His name was Alfred Arthur Rouse.

Rouse had hitched a ride in the cab of the lorry and was dropped off in Cardiff, where he caught a bus to the Welsh pit village of Penbryn.

It was close to eight o'clock in the evening when he arrived in Penbryn. He had gone there to visit Ivy Jenkins, whom he had bigamously married in June 1930. The Jenkins family were of the opinion that Rouse was a good man, and honest and caring about Ivy. They also believed he was in the process of purchasing a house in Kingston for himself and Ivy to move to.

Arriving at the Jenkins's home, he told the family that the journey had taken him eighteen hours to complete. He had stopped off in Northampton, where his car had been stolen, so he had to hitch a lift. Rouse played the part very well and no one seemed to be suspicious of his story. However, his deceit was about to be uncovered.

The *Daily Sketch* of the following day ran a photograph alongside a news story that discussed a burnt-out car that had been discovered in Northampton with human remains inside it. The photograph clearly displayed the registration number MU1468. The family recognised the registration plate and alerted Rouse that his car had been found in Northampton with a body inside. Callously, Rouse refused to accept that it was his car and wanted them to ignore the matter completely. This reaction aroused some concerns in the Jenkins family. Rouse's response was not acceptable and they asked him to contact the police to let them know he was alive and well. In an attempt to appease them, he visited a local police station to report the matter, and there he was told by a local constable to return to London at once.

A neighbour, Mr Brownhill, took Rouse to Cardiff, where the killer took a bus to London. The Welsh police conveyed the information to Scotland Yard and Northampton police that Rouse was making his way back to London on a coach bound for Hammersmith Broadway. As the coach pulled into its destination, police were awaiting him. Alighting, Rouse was at once approached by an officer who asked him to identify himself. 'Alfred Arthur Rouse. I am glad it is all over.' he exclaimed. 'I am glad it is all over, I was going to Scotland Yard. I'm responsible.'

Alfred Arthur Rouse was taken to Hammersmith police station and subsequently interviewed by detectives who wanted to know just what he was responsible for! The travelling salesman talked freely and openly. However, he consistently changed his story and altered his statements. The interviewing officers were amazed about his talkative manner, but soon became perplexed by his rambling tales, which failed to stand up to any scrutiny.

The next morning he was taken to Angel Lane police station in Northampton, where Inspector Lawrence asked for the prisoner to be brought to his office. The Inspector was completing some associated documentation and wanted to form his own opinion about what it was that made Rouse tick, and to ascertain just which details were accurate and which weren't.

Inspector Lawrence explained to Rouse that he was still under caution. However, he was completing some documentation and told Rouse that he could to talk to him if he wanted to, especially about the reasons behind the crime and the identity of the victim.

It didn't take long before Rouse was pacing up and down the Inspector's office discussing his past and filling in the background to the case. It is unlikely that Rouse was totally oblivious to the fact that Lawrence was writing down what he was saying; it is more likely that he was clearing his own conscience and interweaving fact with fiction. In essence, Rouse told Lawrence that he was on 'friendly terms' with several women, but it was an expensive game. One such quote about these friendships has attached itself to the case ever since and was damning evidence at his subsequent trial: 'My harem takes me to several places, and I'm not at home a great deal.'

Background checks were made into the tale told by Rouse. It was quickly ascertained that he did spend a good deal of time away from home. His wife allegedly claimed that, as far as she was concerned or was aware, during such absences he was travelling and working! The

Angel Lane police station, where Rouse was taken on his arrest.

police identified some of the illicit relationships Rouse had spoken of and confirmed that he had fathered at least ten illegitimate children! Worse still, there was a further suggestion that he had admitted to at least eighty relationships during his married life.

With the police file rapidly expanding, more and more information came to light about the remarkable life of deceit Alfred Arthur Rouse had led. He was born in April 1894 and was of Irish descent. He enlisted in the 24th Queen's Territorial Regiment. On 29 November 1914 he had married Lilian May Watkins at St Albans. In March 1914, while still in the armed forces, he was sent to fight in France. Ten days after his arrival he sustained what were described as 'severe' wounds to the head and leg. He returned to England and was taken to Yorkshire for recuperation, eventually being pensioned out of the services in 1916, from which he commenced a career as a travelling salesman.

It was long after his release from the army that he met a fourteen-year-old Helen Campbell, a Scottish girl, whom he duly made pregnant. The child of this relationship was born but died shortly after birth. A friend was able to procure employment for Campbell as a house servant in London, thus allowing Rouse to continue to see and visit her. Two years later, she fell pregnant again. This time, believing him to be divorced from his wife, she insisted that they be married. Rouse agreed and soon the couple made their bogus vows as man and wife. The couple managed to find a flat in Islington where they could live, the problem for Rouse being that he had a real wife living in Friern Barnet! To get round this, he told both women that he would be working away from home a lot of the time as his role had changed and he had a wider area to cover in his capacity as a salesman.

The constant lies and travelling soon made him weary, and eventually he confessed to Helen that he was still married. The young woman was angry and insisted that he tell Lilian about her existence, their relationship and that they had a son (Arthur) of their illicit activities. With no alternatives, he did this and, quite incredibly, both women accepted the fact. Lilian told Helen that it would be best if young Arthur moved in with her, allowing Helen to move on with her own life. Helen agreed and young Arthur moved into the family home in Buxted Road.

There were others too. Nellie Tucker, whom he met in 1925, had two children from her relationship with Rouse. The second was born in the maternity hospital in City Road, London on 29 October 1930, just a few days before Rouse committed his awful act of murder.

The unfortunate woman was spoken to by investigating police officers and informed them that Rouse had visited her around seven o'clock on Bonfire Night 1930. He wasn't his usual confident self and appeared to be very nervous and agitated about something. She had asked him what was troubling him and had been told that he was concerned about his mounting debts and that he did not know which way to turn next. His visit lasted about an hour, and before leaving, he had kissed her goodbye, telling her that he had an appointment up north, which he had to keep. It's easy to see just why Rouse was so agitated: his life had become an inextricable tangle of lies and deceit.

Despite the early failures, the police had been extremely thorough and swift in their investigations. They had the killer under lock and key within thirty-six hours of the crime occurring and had quickly collated sufficient evidence to charge him with murder, although the motive was not quite in place, especially as they had no identity for the unfortunate victim. It was confirmed through medical examination of the remains that the victim was male, but there the information ended.

A check of Rouse's finances produced further evidence, which provided a motive. Shortly before the crime took place, Rouse had increased his insurance cover to provide a policy paying out of £1,000 in the case of death! His assets were nil and clearly the opportunity of receiving such an insurance payout would financially set him up for the rest of his life, £1,000 equating to roughly £200,000 in modern-day values. The one issue the investigating authorities failed to pursue during the investigation was that if Rouse was dead, how was he to cash in his claim? For the first time, here is the only conclusion drawn and determined from all the evidence. Lilian Rouse must have been implicit in the crime, although, as she never made the insurance claim, she never physically committed to her part. The insurance policy document was held at his home address and, prior to leaving home on the night of the crime, Rouse spoke with his wife. Young Arthur told solicitors that he overheard Lilian and Rouse discussing an identification tag and insurance. The identification tag was later found in the burnt-out wreckage. This evidence was never called to court as it was felt that young Arthur had already endured much grief in his life without having to suffer cross-examination in a court of law. Added to this, Lilian would have been the only legal claimant to the insurance.

A committal hearing against Alfred Arthur Rouse was held in Northampton on 16 December 1930. The evidence against the prisoner was offered, including the 'Harem' statement. The defence offered the opinion that such quotes would prejudice the defence, adding that Rouse was being tried for murder and not bigamy. This was duly overruled. The press soon got to know of the 'Harem' evidence and filled their pages with tales of the illustrious love and sex life of the travelling salesman standing trial for murder. There can be no doubt that such stories and coverage did seriously defame the character of the defendant, although the prosecution cleverly did not use or offer the 'Harem' evidence during the trial.

So the trial commenced. Norman Birkett KC, representing the prosecution, called witness after witness who factually vilified Rouse's character. Alfred Brown and Bill Bailey confirmed him as being the man they had seen in Hardingstone Lane on the night of the crime. A representative from the insurance company told how Rouse had taken out extra cover on his vehicle.

Northampton Court, where Rouse was tried.

Lilian Rouse sat facing the dock throughout the trial, the forlorn expression on her face deteriorating as each item of new evidence was introduced. Every so often she would smile at her husband in what was deemed a remarkable display of loyalty. Such was the local feeling for Lilian's position that a local shopkeeper in Bridge Street offered her employment throughout the period of trial to subsidise her expenses, as travelling to and from London each day was expensive. The offer, though a genuine one, was quickly seized on by the media, who pestered the poor woman for stories and opinions. This was good publicity for the shop, but did little to reduce the undoubted stress Mrs Rouse was enduring.

As the trial progressed, the prosecution tightened its grip on the case. Sir Bernard Spilsbury gave evidence as to the injuries sustained by the victim. It was claimed that Rouse had in fact predetermined his victim type. The individual had to be of a similar build and size to himself, perhaps a tramp or vagrant. It was suggested that on his arrival in Hardingstone Lane Rouse rendered the man unconscious outside the car by use of a wooden mallet. He then doused him in petrol from a can which was being carried in the car and which was later found behind the front seat.

Before setting light to the man and the vehicle, he unscrewed the petrol pipe union in the engine, thus causing a flow of petrol and a possible cause or explanation for the car catching fire. With this done, he had then bundled the man into the car across the front seats (hence the awkward position of the body) before setting fire to him. The evidence was tight and clear-cut.

The defence would have none of it. They denied everything that had been suggested. Rouse actually took the witness stand in a desperate attempt to portray a decent image. He spoke of how he had met a stranger at Tally Ho corner. He did not know his name, nor did he enquire what it was. The man was going to the North in search of employment. They had both travelled together to Hardingstone in his car. As they got to Hardingstone Lane, Rouse felt the urge to relieve himself. He asked the stranger to top up the petrol tank by pouring it from the can behind the front seat, while he was relieving himself behind a hedge. He had taken his overnight bag with him as he had noticed the stranger looking at it and he was concerned that if he left it behind the stranger would steal personal effects from it during his absence. While behind the hedge, he heard an explosion and a burst of flames, and looking up, he saw the car was in flames.

> *I ran towards the car, which was in flames. I saw the man inside and tried to open the door but could not as the car was a mass of flames...I was all of a shake. I did not know what to do and ran as hard as I could along the road where I saw two young men...I lost my head and did not know what to do and really don't know what I have done since.*

This was a rational and well-reasoned explanation to the fire and how the man had come to die in the car. However, Birkett was an astute barrister, and was not about to be fooled by the defendant. He asked why Rouse had told lies to the Jenkins family on arrival in Wales and why he took so long to report the matter to the police. Why not report it there and then? Rouse responded, 'In the police's eyes the owner of the car is responsible for anything that happens to that car. Correct me if I am wrong.'

He went on to show little or no emotion for the victim of the fire. Birkett pressed home point after point, asking Rouse how the dead man come to be lying across the front seats with the doors closed if he

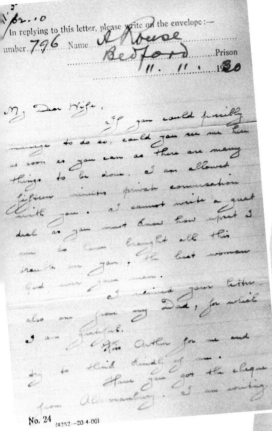

In replying to this letter, please write on the envelope :—
Number 796 Name A Rouse
Bedford Prison
11. 11. 1930

My Dear Wife,

If you could possibly manage to do so, could you see me here as soon as you can as there are many things to be done. I am allowed fifteen minutes private conversation with you. I cannot write a great deal as you must know how upset I am to have brought all this trouble on you, the best woman God ever gave man.

I received your letter, also one from my Dad, for which I am grateful.

Kiss Arthur for me and try to think kindly of me.

Have you got the cheque from Alconbury. I am writing after this to Leicester, to ask them to send to you any money due or about to become due. I should advertise the house for sale as you will want all the money you can get. The insurance on car you cannot touch at all.

However if you can come and see me I will explain all. I cannot eat the food not that it matters much, but you seeing me if you enquire what you can give me you would certainly help my lot here.

Butter is a worse miss. However you had better enquire here first, before seeing me.

Your Husband
Arthur

No. 24 (8252—20-4-00)

H. M. PRISON, Bedford

Nov 11 19 30

Reg. 796 A.A. Rouse.

With reference to the statements as to above-named prisoner's health in the accompanying letter, I have to report that his health is good

Medical Officer.

Forwarded

Governor.

No. 896

A letter written by Rouse from Bedford Prison and a health-check report.

was supposed to be outside filling the car with petrol? Rouse could offer no explanation for this. Birkett then suggested that he must have been in the car with the doors closed when the fire started. Rouse agreed and seemed relieved that the line of questioning had ended, but Birkett fired back, 'How then, was a burnt-off right foot found lying outside the vehicle?' Rouse knew he had been outwitted by the prosecutor and seemed to visibly wilt.

Seizing the opportunity to strike home another fact, Birkett turned to the court and stated that, in his opinion, Rouse had knocked the man unconscious with a wooden mallet which was found close to the car, before bundling him into the car and setting fire to it with a view to making the authorities believe that the burnt remains were those of Alfred Arthur Rouse. The prisoner swayed in the dock and shouted out his denial. He realised, as did everyone in the courtroom that day, that for Alfred Arthur Rouse, the game was up.

At the end of the six-day trial the jury took just one hour and fifteen minutes to reach a unanimous guilty verdict. The judge's clerk placed the black cap on the judge's head. Looking sternly at Rouse, the judge said,

You have been found guilty of this crime for which the law appoints one sentence, and only one, and it is that which I now pronounce on you – that you be taken from hence to the place of lawful execution, and be hanged by the neck until you are dead and that your body be afterwards buried in the precincts of that prison in which you were last confined, and may God have mercy on your soul.

The courtroom was filled with the saddened wails of countless women, including those of Lilian Rouse. As her husband was being led away he turned to look at her. She made an effort to wave but never quite managed to complete the motion before he disappeared from sight, being led down the steps to the cell area. Rouse told his captors that he was innocent and that he loved every woman he had enjoyed sex with. He was taken to Bedford prison, where he was held throughout the trial.

At eight o'clock on the morning of Tuesday, 10 March 1931 at Bedford prison, Alfred Arthur Rouse was hanged. It is said that he was led from the condemned cell to the gallows in a distressed state and was fearful of the fate that awaited him. The final words he uttered were in favour of his wife Lilian, 'Goodbye, dear. You are the best woman I have ever known. I hope the future will hold greater happiness for you.' He pleaded with his executioner to make his exit from this world swift and pain-free; if only he had felt such sympathy for his victim.

The identity of the unknown man has never truly been determined; it is the one secret Rouse took to the grave with him. However, my recent research has revealed a potential identity, that of Cyril Bryce Wilsden, who disappeared around the same time and is believed by his nephew Norman to be yet another victim of Rouse. Certainly, Cyril would have been in the area suggested by Rouse at the time of the murder, and he has not been heard of since.

Whoever the victim was, their remains were given a full Christian burial in Hardingstone village church. At the foot of the simple wooden cross is buried a metal case containing papers and a true and accurate record of how the man died. The cross

Cyril Bryce Wilsden: was he Rouse's victim?

bears the simple inscription, 'In memory of an unknown man. Died Nov 6 1930.'

The Author with John Stalker in a TV documentary on the Rouse case.

Chapter 15

Nailed up in a Boxroom
1938

*Sunday, 21 August 1938 was Higham Ferrers Feast Day.
The tiny Northamptonshire town was packed with
thousands of visitors enjoying the festivities and
trying to forget their gloom about the prospect of war.*

One street in particular had become unusually popular that year as hundreds of folk found time to wander down Wharf Road, stopping outside one house to stare up at the premises. Not that the house was in any way remarkable in appearance; it was a typical small semi-detached home, bearing the name Steeplestone. What made it different to all the others in the street was that it was a murder house. At around 9.50 a.m. on the Saturday morning, Albert Hedley Harrison left his home in Wharf Road and walked to the police station at Rushden. At the main desk he asked to see an inspector and took a seat, and when an officer arrived, asked,

Wharf Road, the area where the murder took place.

You are the inspector? I expect you will soon be wanting me. I wish to tell you I strangled my wife last night. I think you will find her dead. I want you to go before my boy, who is twelve years of age, gets home for dinner.

The Duty Inspector was Robert Valentine, an experienced and respected officer who had worked on a number of murder inquiries. Listening to Harrison, Valentine realised from the man's demeanour that this was no hoax, and no lunatic walking in off the street making rash claims for attention. Valentine had a doctor called and asked that he meet them at the house in Wharf Road. Harrison was placed in a locked cell and the police at once hurried to the scene of the alleged crime. Inside the house bloodstains were evident at the foot of the stairs, and smears and drops of it could be seen on individual stairs leading up to the first-floor landing. Here they stopped at a door, which had been nailed shut. Inspector Valentine felt his heart rate increase as adrenalin pumped around his body. It was clear from all he knew thus far that they would probably fine dead human remains behind the door. Recording in detail the believed crime scene, Valentine ordered the door to be forced open. Sure enough, there they found the body of Mabel Harrison lying on the floor wrapped in a bloodstained sheet. Removing this, the officers noted that her face and head had suffered injuries: bruising, cuts and scratches were clearly evident. A single white bootlace was tightly secured around her throat. This had been tied so tightly that it had cut into the surface skin of the neck, causing some light bleeding and ligature marks.

The crime scene secured, a police officer was detailed to stand at the front of the house to prevent unauthorised access. Valentine, meanwhile, returned to Rushden police station, where he briefed Superintendent Williams of the facts of the case. The senior officer at once cautioned and charged Albert Harrison with murder. The accused responded, 'I am truly sorry I did it. She was not the same woman I once knew and married, I would never have hurt that woman.' Williams then secured a full and detailed statement of confession from Harrison.

In Wharf Road, inquisitive neighbours began to flock around the front of the house; it was then that the scurrilous rumours and gossip started. Stories of how Albert Harrison had been a loyal and loving husband and father circulated. His wife, however, was regarded locally as something of a scarlet woman. Out gallivanting with other men until all hours, she was a regular at local dances and in public houses. Indeed, further tales about her promiscuity at her place of work in Raunds were bandied about, and from all that was being said, Mabel Harrison appeared to have been leading a dual life. From the outset, despite anyone truly knowing the circumstances or what had happened, all the sympathy was with Albert.

A detailed police examination of the inside of the house in Wharf Road took place, and a second white bootlace exactly matching the one round the dead woman's neck was found in a football boot in an outhouse; the other boot was minus a lace! When the search for evidence was complete, the final remains of Mabel Harrison were removed from the house. A small band of local people witnessed the event and there was some crying and wailing, as the speculation reached a crescendo. 'Murder, it was murder!' they shouted. 'He's killed her, good on him too. Did he stab her?' Much of the population of Higham Ferrers was playing its own murder mystery game, but sadly for the victim few gave her a second thought; all the concern was for Albert and his two boys! The body was taken to the Wellingborough police station mortuary, where it was later formally identified as Mabel Annie Harrison by Abraham Cook, the father of the dead woman.

A special court hearing was held in Higham Ferrers town hall that same afternoon, requesting authorisation for Harrison to remain in custody pending further inquiries. The scene outside the town hall was quiet. No one other than the police knew of Albert's whereabouts. In the distance, music and the sound of merriment could be heard from the nearby fair. Albert walked solemnly into the building, flanked all the time by two plain-clothes police officers. He was remanded for further questioning in a hearing which lasted just a few minutes, and was then conveyed to Wellingborough police station for further questioning.

Albert Harrison was held in a cell for a further week and made his first public appearance in court the following week. Crowds of people lined the street cheering and waving their support for him. It was an incredible scene that was unprecedented anywhere in the county. Inside Higham Ferrers town hall, while the court waited for the magistrates to arrive, a further curious but genuine thing happened. Mabel Harrison's white-haired father walked up to Albert in court and shook him firmly by the hand. He then sat beside the prisoner talking to him. There was no animosity, in fact, precisely the opposite. At the hearing Harrison was remanded in custody and granted legal aid.

Many employees at his place of work set up an appeal to raise funds to hire the services of a renowned criminal lawyer. They couldn't have chosen better. Mr Norman Birkett KC was simply the best there was at that time. Controversial and meticulous in his examination and case preparation, Birkett had an awesome reputation in court. Unconcerned about his fees, Birkett was still probably relieved to find out how popular Albert was locally. In Higham Ferrers itself some 7,000 people, many of them members of the Boot Operatives Union, to which Harrison belonged, contributed to the £250 fee.

Slowly the issues surrounding the case were becoming clear. Albert Harrison and Mabel had married in 1918, and had two sons, Keith, aged twelve, and Clifford aged eighteen. At the time of the murder, Clifford was away from home on holiday. The couple were employed in the shoemaking industry, working in different factories. Mabel earned about 30 shillings a week, which allowed her freedom and some independence. Regularly she would go out with friends socialising, particularly on Friday and Saturday nights. Poor Albert, meanwhile, would remain at home looking after the children. It appears that at no time did he suspect his wife of being unfaithful to him: why should he? She assured him that she went out with her other women friends, and he believed her. Mabel was also an active member of the Salvation Army and was by all accounts a well-known figure in the town when wearing her uniform.

The Wednesday before her death, as she did with increasing frequency, Mabel had gone out after work. She told her husband that she was going to see a solicitor about personal business (just why such a visit should be acceptable to Albert was never clarified). She returned home late and slept in a separate bedroom to her husband. This was unusual but this too had happened more frequently in recent weeks.

The following day, Thursday, 18 August, Albert was visited at his place of work by Mrs Grace Talbot, who asked him where his wife had been on the Wednesday of a fortnight earlier. Thinking, Albert told the woman that she had travelled to London to watch the Changing of the Guard with a woman friend. Mrs Talbot informed him otherwise, assuring him that her own husband, who actually worked with Mabel, had also gone to see the Changing of the Guard that day, and also that the two of them had been having a love affair for a period of over a year. The couple had made time for one another, their special time together being at 1.10 p.m. each day.

Albert was mortified. He could sense his world collapsing around him. He needed privacy to take in the news, and so asked Mrs Talbot to leave him, arranging with her to visit Steeplestone that evening so that she could confront Mabel Harrison in front of him. Albert couldn't believe the love of his life had, if the Talbot woman was right, betrayed him.

Grace Talbot did as she was asked and visited the house in Wharf Road later. Almost on sight she accused Mabel of going on her trip to London with her husband. Mabel, surprised no doubt, retaliated and vehemently denied the allegation. She became violent towards Albert, verbally abusing him and kicking him hard on his shin. Albert had become emotional and asked his wife to calm down and tell him it was untrue, all lies: she couldn't, and didn't!

A bitter argument ensued, and in Mrs Talbot's own words, 'Mabel Harrison became very nasty'. Albert Harrison, in contrast, was constantly trying to be reasonable and displayed no sign of violence or aggression towards his wife. Eventually, getting nowhere, Mrs Talbot left the couple, advising them as she did that it was her intention to see a solicitor about a divorce and to name Mabel Harrison as co-respondent in the matter.

The following day, Friday, Albert, devastated by the news and situation with his wife, stayed away from work. His official statement was honest and clear. It read:

On Friday 19th August I got up at 6.15 a.m. to see my boy off to work. My wife then got up at 7.30 a.m. and cut some lunch for herself. She then went to work. I did not go to work that day as I felt very much upset but I went to Raunds and asked a mate to collect my wages for me. My wife came home at 5.30 p.m. I had a kettle of boiling water on the gas. My wife emptied it into a jug and said, 'I am going to see him tonight.' I believe she meant Talbot. I said 'You are not'. With that she started to

The Wheatsheaf Inn, *where Harrison drank after his crime.*

run upstairs and fell on the bottom step, striking her eye, and shouting abuse at me. I went for her and she must have turned round as she scratched my face on the left side, and while she lay there I put my hands around her neck. She did not struggle much, and I pulled a lace from my pocket and tied it around her neck. I was very much upset at the time and could not have been responsible for my actions as I loved my wife and there was no other woman in the world for me.

By this time it was around 6.30 p.m. I carried her to what we call the boxroom. I saw there was some blood on the stair carpet, bannister and a little on the wall. I washed it off as well as I could with some clothing which I put in the box room. Feeling sure my wife was dead I nailed up the door so that my boy should not go in. I then washed and changed my clothes, locked up the house and went to Rushden to meet my mate with my wages. I left home at about 7.30 p.m., meeting my mate at 8 p.m., with whom I went for a drink of beer in the Wheatsheaf *public house. I bought a quartern of whisky and a small bottle of beer to take home with me. I returned home after collecting my son from the fair, and we went to bed sleeping in separate rooms. My son never asked where his mother was.*

The next morning I got up at 5.30 a.m., got my boy's breakfast and later came to Rushden police station and told the Police what I had done.

On Wednesday, 24 August the remains of Mabel Annie Harrison were interred at the Wellingborough–Doddington Road cemetery. An estimated crowd of 800 people attended as the deceased was laid to rest. The mood was sombre, and thankfully, full respect was shown. Most of those attending were work colleagues, and there was a wide array of wreaths and bouquets of flowers, but there was one notable absentee from the affair: her husband.

Two months later, Norman Birkett appeared for the defence in a murder trial which took place at the Northampton Assizes and lasted just one hour and six minutes. At precisely 11.19 a.m., Albert Hedley Harrison stood in the dock, wearing a smart blue suit and a black tie. There was a sincere sense of sadness in the courtroom that day. Those in the public gallery anticipated a grave outcome to the proceedings, and rightly so, after all Albert had killed his wife.

Killer Albert Harrison.
Victim Mabel Harrison.

Albert pleaded not guilty to the charge of murder; a plea thoroughly supported by virtually everyone in the court that day. Mr Maurice Healy, prosecuting, provided a fine opening speech, expounding Albert's previously good character and how in the circumstances he had killed his wife in such a way as to justify the reduction of the verdict to one of manslaughter. He went on to explain that Albert was in fact the unfortunate victim of circumstances, his wife had never truly been faithful to him, in fact, she had been involved in an illicit relationship six years previously. This, it was revealed, had come to Albert's attention at the time, yet he chose to ignore or forget it in the hope that the love of his life would change her ways. Leopards, as they say, rarely change their spots!

Meanwhile, Norman Birkett took the floor in defence of his client. In an absolutely remarkable few minutes, he had the public gallery in tears and the accused in the dock breaking down in an unforgettable outburst of tears and pleas for forgiveness. Birkett loved playing to an audience and he was at his theatrical best in this case. Every opportunity to elicit sympathy was grasped as the already poor reputation of Mabel Annie Harrison was further tarnished with the suggestion of a string of other lovers. He further explained that he would allow his client to plead guilty to manslaughter but not to murder. Mr Justice Oliver asked the prosecution if they had any real objection to the proposal suggested by the defence team. None was forthcoming and the Crown overwhelmingly concurred with the defence counsel on a charge of manslaughter.

Birkett continued his closing speech;

The man realises and recognises that there must be punishment. In one sense no punishment that you, your Lordship, could inflict could ever be heavier than the punishment that this man now bears. The remorse, the contrition, will remain with him for all time. All I can do is to say here is a tragic and sad case, the law itself is merciful, but over and above that mercy is the prerogative of this court, and I ask you, having regard to your public duty and the unique circumstances, to treat this man mercifully and as leniently as you can. It is not a case where deterrent is concerned. I commend this unfortunate man to your Lordship's most merciful consideration.

There can be no doubting that Mr Justice Oliver himself was moved by the entire case. In his closing speech he said;

It seems terrible to me to prolong an investigation of this sort which can only have one result. I am weak enough to wish that the task of dealing with you had fallen on to any judge but me, there are circumstances for which you are not in the least to be blamed and over which you had no control, but I am bound to administer the law. I have weighed every word your counsel has said – there is no man at the Bar who could have said it better. The least I can possibly sentence you to is three years penal servitude.

On hearing the punishment, Albert burst into tears in the dock. He was a broken man, his life all but destroyed by the actions of a woman who could not return his loyalty and devotion; a woman who abused his generous affection. However, for such ingratitude nobody deserves to die. Sadly, in this case Mabel Harrison was an unfortunate victim.

Chapter 16

The Rushden Tragedy
1942

Money can't buy you everything, especially loyalty,
happiness and true love.
Just who killed whom in Rushden?

A rthur Clifford Sumpter was by trade a bootmaker who had grown up with his family roots in the industry. He was forced to leave the occupation and enlist in the armed forces during the First World War. He was immediately sent overseas, and while in armed combat he sustained an injury, which forced him to return to England for medical treatment, and for some time he was in a hospital in Newcastle upon Tyne. While recuperating there in St James's hospital, he became friendly with a colliery owner by the name of Embleton, who was also being treated for war injuries. Through the injuries he received, Sumpter was eventually discharged from the services and duly left hospital. He returned to Rushden, where he had no option but to resume work in the bootmaking industry.

Unexpectedly, some time in 1930, he received information through his solicitors that his hospital friend, Mr Embleton, had passed away, leaving him somewhere in the region of £30,000 in his last will and testament. Arthur Sumpter was taken aback by this wonderful gesture, but nevertheless graciously accepted the money and at once resigned from his position as a bootmaker. Without further hesitation he purchased a bigger house on the Bedford Road, in Rushden. A bachelor, the house he purchased was a little on the large size for a lone gentleman, and required maintenance and upkeep which he didn't quite fancy doing himself. So, with this in mind, he invited his sister and brother-in-law, Frederick James Tyman, to live with him. The couple were then effectively employed to act as cook and gardener in lieu of payment for their accommodation.

A handsome man, Arthur Sumpter was not unable to attract women friends. He apparently had a reputation locally as a friendly yet deep and broody character, a man who would enjoy a social drink in the pub but also enjoyed a tipple in the privacy of his own home. In June 1941 Sumpter employed a young woman whom he had been attracted to on one of his local social expeditions, to act as his housekeeper. Her name was Betty Gallay. The young woman was bowled over by the handsome Sumpter and almost immediately moved into the house, where, before long, she was living with Sumpter as his partner and lover, in what some local people described as a 'man and wife' relationship. The situation was not to the Tymans' liking; they felt it shameful that their relative should allow the young woman such freedom so quickly. Not surprisingly, they opted to move out of the house, taking temporary accommodation elsewhere in the town. Despite this, each morning Frederick Tyman would return to the Sumpter home, make the couple a pot of tea and some light breakfast, which he would take to the upstairs bedrooms. This done, he would then carry out general household duties and tend to the garden. Sumpter and Gallay got to the stage where they seem to have lost all respect for Tyman. They would lounge about in bed all day, abusing Frederick Tyman's goodwill and treating him as a servant or butler.

By mid-December 1942, Betty Gallay had built a good relationship with Frederick Tyman and saw him as something of a confidant. She would tell him of the tempestuous rows she was having with Sumpter, who had become possessive and jealous. One particular row of note occurred when she had mentioned how a soldier friend had visited the house in his absence. Arthur had gone mad and seemingly made all kinds of threats of violence against her. The quarrelling continued after this, and on Christmas Day 1942, Betty actually told Frederick that the relationship with Arthur was over and that her friendship with the soldier had progressed. She now intended to marry him as soon as it was possible. Deeply concerned about the situation, Frederick expressed his concern about how Arthur would react when told this news; Betty at once allayed all such fears by informing him that Sumpter already knew and had accepted it.

Thursday, 31 December 1942 was typically cold and damp. For Frederick Tyman it was his usual routine. At about 8.00 a.m. he arrived at the Sumpter house, made the morning tea and took it upstairs to them both. Peering through the open door of Betty Gallay's room, he saw the couple lying on the double bed. He lightly tapped on the bedroom door but received no response. Believing that they had been out drinking the night before, he thought it may be best to leave them to sleep it off, so left the tray outside the room on the landing floor. He went downstairs, carried out some chores and went out into the garden, where he cleared off some of the general garden detritus that had fallen from trees or been carried in on the wind.

It was cold so he didn't waste much time in the garden, and returned indoors and went back upstairs with further refreshments. To his surprise the couple were still lying on the bed and hadn't moved. Tentatively he pushed open the bedroom door and slowly walked in, calling out both Arthur's and Betty's names as he did so. Neither of them stirred. As he approached the bed he could see the couple both lying on their backs. Betty had her mouth wide open. Something was wrong.

Now worried, Tyman bent over Betty Gallay and gently squeezed her hand in an attempt to awaken her. He recoiled in horror, as her hand was cold and rigid from the onset of rigor mortis. Looking around he saw a revolver by Arthur's right leg. It was clear that what he was looking at was a case of murder. He falsely believed that both parties had been shot and killed by some unknown assailant. Leaving the room with some haste, he went downstairs and called the police.

At 10.00 a.m. the same morning, Detective Inspector H. J. Lee and Sergeant Tansley of the Northamptonshire Constabulary arrived at the house. The sergeant was to record the crime scene in his pocket book:

> The black-out curtains in the room were drawn and the light was on. There was no sign of a struggle and Gallay lay on her back with her arms folded over her chest. Sumpter was also on his back with his head resting on the woman's shoulder. Two inches from his right hand was a .38 Service Enfield revolver.

The police made a call for a doctor's attendance and soon Dr O. B. Lean of Rushden arrived. He certified Betty Gallay as life extinct (dead), having been so for an estimated six hours. However, on examining Arthur Sumpter he found signs of life. He was alive, and while that was the case, he was potentially a key witness to proceedings. The injured man was at once conveyed to Northampton General Hospital, accompanied by Sergeant Tansley. The police officer's journey was a futile one. He was not to get the opportunity to ascertain any detail from the wounded man, as he died without uttering another word.

Dr Lean made a cursory examination of the remains of Betty Gallay at the scene. This revealed four separate bullet wounds to her body, three of which were in her chest region. The other was in her arm. Any of the chest wounds could have been fatal. With forensic science literally unheard of it was impossible for the investigating authorities to ascertain whether she had been shot while sleeping or while awake, although there seemed to have been little or no sign of any struggle or defensive action from the deceased, so it seemed that she had been shot while in her sleep. Meanwhile, at Northampton General Hospital, two bullet wounds were found on the body of Arthur Sumpter. One was in his right temple, the other in his left shoulder. The fatal shot was confirmed as being located in the temple region.

Back in Bedford Road, the police carried out door-to-door inquiries asking if anyone had seen anything suspicious or witnessed any strangers loitering in the area. No one had seen or heard anything. A thorough search of the house revealed no sign of a break-in, and with the assistance of Frederick Tyman it was ascertained that nothing appeared to be missing from the house, thus ruling out a break in or a burglary. The revolver found at the scene was confirmed as belonging to Arthur Sumpter. This had been removed from its usual position in the wardrobe in his bedroom.

Slowly but surely the police pieced together what evidence they had in preparation for the inquest, which was held at Wellingborough Petty Sessional Court, on Saturday, 6 January 1943. East Northants Coroner Mr J. Cairns-Parker was presiding officer. As each witness came forward with background information an intriguing tale of love and, sadly, jealousy, emerged.

Mrs Laura Barratt told the court how Betty Gallay was in fact her daughter; her real name was not Gallay but Betty Margaret Barratt. The name Gallay was something she had adopted herself some time previously. Betty was twenty-four years old at the time of her death.

Mrs Barratt continued bravely with her evidence and spoke of a particularly chilling tale told to her by her daughter a few days before her death. Apparently, after a serious quarrel with Sumpter, Betty had left the house for a short time to allow the situation to calm down. On her return she found a handwritten note from Arthur that stated that first he would shoot her and later, kill himself! The police were never able to ascertain the full accuracy of this anecdotal evidence as the note was never recovered or located. However, it seemed to fit with all the facts of the case rather too well for it to be totally inaccurate.

Detective Inspector Lee gave evidence and was asked to provide what the police by virtue of their investigation had theoretically assessed to be the full scenario surrounding the build-up and actual committal of the crime on the night and morning in question.

The couple had been sighted drinking in a public house in Wymington (a village not far from their home) at around 10.00 p.m. on the night of 30 December 1942. Both were said by those who saw them to be merry and in good spirit. There was no obvious outward sign of any problem between them. It was believed that, on returning home together and with the 44-year-old Sumpter in good humour, Betty Gallay seized the opportunity to invite Arthur into her room (they had separate bedrooms) and tell him of her relationship with the soldier and her intention to marry him.

Arthur Sumpter had seemed to calmly accept the tale and invited Gallay onto the bed, where they both drank a measure of neat whisky. Eventually, now drowsy, Gallay lay down on the bed and possibly asked Sumpter to leave, as she was feeling tired. Sumpter, it would appear, did as he was asked.

On arrival in his own room he was seething with rage and jealousy, and there he took out the service revolver from its place in the wardrobe and went to bed. Minutes later, he would return to Gallay's room armed with the revolver and fire shots into her resting body. He had then climbed onto the bed beside her and shot himself.

To support this case, the Inspector provided corroborating evidence in the form of handwritten letters belonging to Gallay, which tended to prove that it was her intention to marry the soldier in the near future. Furthermore, cartridges of exactly the same type as those in Sumpter's revolver were found by the body of Gallay. A further twenty-four identical cartridges were found in his wardrobe, thus linking the murder weapon directly to him.

The Coroner was succinct in his summing-up and advised the jury that they must decide whether the Inspector and the authorities were correct in their assumptions. However, as there was not a solitary witness to the crime itself, they were no more than assumptions. It has to be said that,

The pub in Wymington where Sumpter and Gallay were last seen alive.

on this occasion, the accepted facts of the case more or less dictated that the investigating authorities were accurate and thus correct. Certainly no evidence to the contrary was found or was ever forthcoming. All that remained was a final verdict of murder then suicide.

Despite the verdict, a number of questions remained unanswered in this case, among them: What was it that finally drove Sumpter to murder? Was it simply the jealous reaction of a spurned lover, or was it, as Laura Barratt's evidence seemed to indicate, a case of premeditated murder? What of the bullet wound to his left shoulder?

In answer to the last question, it seems highly likely that Arthur Clifford Sumpter was heavily under the influence of alcohol at the time of the crime. Perhaps he panicked when trying to end his life with a gunshot. Possibly judging that he was shooting directly into his heart, yet in his drunken state he missed, so opted for the second shot, this time to the head. We shall never truly know.

There are tales locally that the mysterious 'unnamed' soldier was himself a married man who was having an extra-marital affair with Betty Gallay. This would account for why the authorities maintained discretion concerning his actual identity throughout the investigation and inquiry. Whatever the case, it matters little now. This sad situation caused unnecessary despair in two, perhaps three families, the mysterious local soldier being the third casualty because he lost the object of his desire and affection.

Chapter 17

Red Herrings, Intrigue and a Mystery 1952

*A picturesque village in rural Northamptonshire
is suddenly thrust into the notoriety of an unsolved murder –
that is, until now?*

The picturesque village of Ashton is tucked away in the north-east of the county. It is situated on the edge of Ashton Wold, very close to Oundle. In more recent times it is more commonly known as the home of the World Conker Championships, which take place on its village green every year. In 1903, Lord Nathaniel Charles Rothschild had all the cottages built to house the workforce who were employed on his rambling estate. Since then it has altered very little in its appearance. It consists of just thirty-two thatched cottages. There is also a pub in the village – the *Three Horseshoes*.

Back in 1952, the era with which we are concerned, the Rothschild estate was managed by the Honourable Mrs George Lane (née Miriam Louisa Rothschild) and her husband, of Polish descent, Captain George Lane (previously Lanyi). The couple had married on 14 August 1943 and had, by 1952, four children: Mary Rozsiska, Charles Daniel, Charles Theresa and Johanna Miriam Lane. Together the Lane family lived in the beautiful ivy-clad family home called 'Ashton Wold'.

Ashton was in 1952 an extremely close-knit community, with so few homes and just one road running directly through the village, there seemed to be no escape from the gaze of one's neighbours. It has been said to me that if something happened at one end of the village, the people at the opposite end would know about it in minutes. To the outside world the agreed general perception of Ashton back in the

1950s was one of a blissful environment, a quiet, sedate location with no apparent jealousy or ill feeling among those who lived in its community.

George and Lillian Peach lived in a secluded cottage, at the far end of the village, which was known locally as 'West Lodge' or the 'Oats House'. It was precisely 480 yards from the nearest cottage in the village, so it was somewhat removed from the often prying eyes of neighbours or village life. The couple had moved to Ashton in the spring of 1946. George Peach, who was sixty-four years old, and was more commonly referred to locally as 'Harry', worked on the estate as gamekeeper and handyperson. His wife, Lillian, was sixty-seven years of age and was an unassuming sort of woman who made friends easily but generally kept herself to herself, much preferring the solitude of West Lodge to the more active life in the centre of the village.

Generally speaking, the couple certainly appeared to be liked by virtually all the community and outwardly there was no one who seemed to have a serious dislike of them. Yes, at times George could be inquisitive and interfering, but that was just his way. He had worked hard on the land for much of his life, carrying out virtually all the tasks (tasks that now took two people to undertake) single-handedly. He liked to see things done properly and was always keen to lend a helping hand. This genuine show of enthusiasm was not always appreciated and it is known he had a couple of minor altercations with some of the farmhands and labourers, but these always seemed to be amicably resolved.

At 4.25 p.m. on Friday, 24 October 1952, George Peach said goodbye to his old friend Walter Brundell in the village. Both men had finished a day's work and were on their way home. Lillian Peach was seen hanging washing out at the cottage at around 5.00 p.m. the same evening. These were the last sightings of the couple alive.

The following morning, butcher's boy Lawrence Wright drove his van up to West Lodge to deliver the Peaches' Sunday joint. He pushed open the tiny wooden gate and walked up the path of the front garden round the side of the house to the rear access wooden kitchen door. Unusually, this was locked, so he knocked loudly in the hope of attracting one of the occupants' attention. There was no reply so he decided to take the joint down to the *Three Horseshoes* public house on the village green, and leave it with Mrs Slater, the wife of the licensee.

As he made his way back to his van at the front of the house, Wright noticed that all the downstairs curtains were drawn across. Not unnaturally, he thought the couple must have overslept. On leaving the meat with the Slaters, he returned to the butcher's shop in Oundle.

In the pub, landlord Frank Slater had some concerns about George and Lillian. He had heard that George had failed to arrive for work that morning, which was suspicious as, generally, he was one of the first in. This, added to the fact that all the downstairs curtains were drawn closed and there was no reply to a call at the house, made him worried.

Dutifully, Slater made his way over to the farm manager's office at Chapel Farm, and asked John Dockray if he knew anything about George's non-attendance at work that morning. The farm manager knew nothing and, from what we know, didn't seem unduly concerned by the matter. Slater asked if he would come with him to West Lodge to check on the old couple. Dockray declined to do so but said his secretary could go. Arriving at the house, Frank Slater entered the house by the closed but unlocked front door, and as he did so, called out the couple's names. There was no reply.

Climbing through the darkness of the staircase, he arrived on the first-floor landing. He peered through the dull light that had managed to find its way through the closed curtains in the first bedroom. He was unprepared for the scene he was about to witness. He jumped with shock when he saw, lying on the bed, covered in blood, Lillian Peach. He could see that she was unconscious, as she wouldn't respond to her name. The poor publican was mortified but noticed that she was still breathing in an agitated manner. He at once fled downstairs and returned with some haste to Chapel Farm, where he called local police. The estate chauffeur was present in the office when the call was made, and as he was qualified in first aid, he returned to the grim scene with Frank Slater. Both men entered Lillian's bedroom, where they covered her body to keep her warm until the emergency services arrived.

The men were concerned about where George Peach was, as there was no sign of him in the bedroom. Quietly they moved across the landing to another bedroom, but looking in they found it empty. The third and final bedroom door was closed. Both men knew that George was probably in there. Tentatively, the chauffeur tried the handle. It was locked. The chauffeur managed to force open the door with his shoulder, and it swung wide open. Both men stared in horror. George Peach lay in his bed with the bedclothes still pulled up around his neck, his head and neck being the only visible parts. He lay on his back with his head angled to the left. A large amount of blood was visible on the left side of his face and head, and on the pillow. The chauffeur approached the man. It was clear he was dead and had been for some time, from the onset of rigor mortis. Curiously, there was no sign of the bedroom door key on the inside of the lock or anywhere in the bedroom, yet it had been locked.

Just after 11.00 a.m. a doctor arrived and certified George Peach dead. He instructed a police officer to transfer Lillian to Peterborough Hospital as her body had gone into complete shock and her condition was life-threatening. Inspector Harold Peel and Constable Moriarty of the Northamptonshire Constabulary also arrived on scene. The investigating officers noted that a small rear pantry window was open, one of its tiny leaded panes absent, allowing hand access for the opening and securing of the window. This appeared to be the obvious point of access. There was no other obvious evidence of anything out of the ordinary throughout the downstairs rooms of the house.

Soon there was an assembled throng of senior police officers at West Lodge. The instruction for the whole area to be sealed off was given and no access or egress from the village was permitted without prior police knowledge and approval. The murder investigation had now begun.

At Peterborough Hospital, Lillian Peach quietly passed away at 7.45 p.m. the same evening, without regaining consciousness, so she could not provide any further clues to what had taken place in her home. It was now a double murder inquiry, so at this point in the investigation the decision to call in Scotland Yard was taken. The officers from the metropolis arrived in Oundle at 11.00 p.m. that evening and at once took the lead role in the investigation. In Ashton, the villagers were quiet; extremely quiet. There was now some reluctance to discuss anything about the couple from West Lodge, perhaps through fear of false incrimination, perhaps for more sinister reasons.

Whatever the situation in the village, the Lane family were more than helpful and provided some background information about the dead couple. It transpired that they had a son, Jack, who lived and worked in Staines, Middlesex. Jack Peach was unaware of the situation regarding his parents until about 7.00 p.m. on Saturday, 25 October, when officers from the Metropolitan police called at his home to break the sad news to him. The son had last seen his parents alive in mid-August 1952 when they travelled to Middlesex to see and stay with him and his wife for six days. The poor man had the woeful task of travelling to the Glapthorne Road mortuary, Oundle, to formally identify the battered remains of his parents.

Scotland Yard detectives commenced inquiries in Ashton, as they desperately sought a motive for this awful crime. It was ascertained that George Peach had received his pay-packet on Friday, 24 October, containing the sum of £0 13s 6d for that particular week. It was clear that he had had no opportunity to spend any of this money, yet no sign of his pay-packet or the money was to be found.

A formal post-mortem was held on both bodies by Professor J. M. Webster of the Forensic Science Laboratory, Birmingham. It was quickly ascertained that George Peach had sustained in the region of thirteen separate blows to his head and neck area. As a result of the severity and power of these blows his skull had been fractured in several places. Lillian Peach had suffered, too. There were at least four identifiable fractures to her skull as she had moved her head in an attempt to avoid the blows. Along with this there was clear evidence of self-defence wounds on her right arm and left hand where she had tried to defend herself using her arms, again against the blows. From the state of the wounds and clear, round image of the skull fractures, Professor Webster confirmed that the most likely weapon used in the attack was some form of flat-headed hammer. The Professor gave the estimated time of death of George Peach as between the hours of 1.00 a.m. and 2.00 a.m. on the morning of 25 October 1952. At last the police had something to work with. The potential time of the attack on the couple would allow some progress to be made.

More than thirty constables from the Northamptonshire Constabulary were called in to carry out a sweep search of the entire village from West Lodge down to the Polebrook Road access point to the village. The murder weapon and the key to George Peach's bedroom door were still missing and could potentially hold vital forensic evidence if located quickly. From the size of the wounds to the skull it was established that the murder weapon was a coal hammer, a tool that every home in Ashton would possess to crack down blocks of coal, which was then the primary source of household fuel available to the community.

In a solid line the police officers sifted through wooded areas, gardens, ditches and dykes, leaving no area for error. Virtually every blade of grass and leaf was moved in the search for clues and evidence. Nothing was located, no coal hammer, no key. As a result of this the investigating detectives believed the killer must have taken the murder weapon away from the village.

For the police there was complete embarrassment when, at around 3.05 p.m. on 1st November, the Oundle police station control room received a call from Mrs Marsh, a resident of Ashton village, stating that she had found a bloodstained coal hammer in the cabbage patch in her garden – an area which had previously been covered in the police search! Superintendent Wilfred Tarr of Scotland Yard took possession of the hammer. It transpired that Mrs Marsh's daughter had lost a ring in the garden and while searching for this had found the object among fallen cabbage leaves. Its head had been facing away from the boundary wall that ran alongside and fronted the main road through the village.

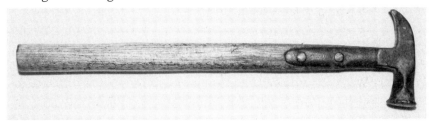

The murder weapon: a coal hammer.

Matted hair and congealed blood on the head of the hammer was identified; this was indeed the murder weapon. The killer had then made his way back through the village and tossed the weapon over the garden wall on the way; a somewhat outrageous act if the killer was a stranger to the area? To have in your possession a bloodstained murder weapon when entering a central village area, at any time of day or night, would leave you exposed to detection if you should happen to be seen by anyone! The hammer was found about 600 yards from West Lodge, and at least fourteen occupied residences had to be walked past on this journey, making it seem all the more reckless for a stranger who would, to put it bluntly, stick out like a sore thumb. The police realised this, too, but the last thing they needed was to cause problems in the local community that might cause the locals to close ranks and clam up.

The movements of known local vagrants and alien workers were sought. Nearby was Polebrook Workers hospital, whose residents included Polish and other foreign nationals. One such individual was Nikolaus Skoropei, a 27-year-old Ukrainian who has been proposed by one theorist as a potential suspect. Certainly, for a while the police were interested in Skoropei. He had been away from his place of residence most of the night on the night of the murder, and he told a lie to a fellow-worker at the Molesworth camp to borrow a bicycle. He had taken five hours to get home, walking past the access road to Ashton on the way.

The police investigated his story. He claimed he had gone to Oundle, visited every pub in the main street then gone to a dance in the Drill Hall, before returning home and having to walk and push the borrowed bicycle, as the chain had broken. The story was corroborated and was true. Skoropei was also at the time in question the worse for alcohol. He would never have been able to force entry through the tiny pantry window of West Lodge without making a noise. That aside, he would have to pass through the centre of the village twice to get to and from West Lodge; hardly feasible in his drunken state. So there is no sudden end to the mystery at this point in the investigation.

While the press of the day stated that over 500 people had been interviewed and spoken to by police, it was in fact closer to three thousand. Some two thousand fingerprints were taken (all male) in an attempt to identify an alien print found on the beading of the rear pantry window of West lodge. The reality was that the print was potentially old and could have been an innocent rogue print with a trace left there. No unidentified prints were found in West Lodge, so it is more likely that the killer would have worn protective gloves to prevent identification. The end result of this comprehensive search was that no fingerprint match was found.

The usual flurry of random associated reports came flooding into the police incident room; a lorry driver travelling towards Wellingborough on the A605 road was nearing Oundle when he saw a group of about six people in the road. One, a female aged about forty to forty-five, appeared agitated and ran into the road, seemingly trying to stop the lorry. The driver took evasive action and continued on his way, a little unnerved but feeling that the people seemed desperate for a lift. The question is, was it an attempt to extricate themselves from the area as soon as possible? The group was never located.

A railway porter from Peterborough North station reported two suspicious men; they had arrived at the railway station around 2.15 a.m. on the morning of the murder, boarding the London-bound train. The men apparently had flushed complexions, and one had a handkerchief tied round his left wrist with blood seeping through the temporary bandage. Peterborough is about twelve miles from Ashton. How did the men get there, did they walk or run, or get a lift? And why were their complexions still flushed? Again, neither man was traced.

More confusing and time-consuming incidents transpired. For instance, the police had announced to the press that George Peach's pocket-watch may be missing and had possibly been removed from the house. An accurate description of the said timepiece was recorded from an Oundle jeweller who had repaired the watch during the summer of 1952. The description was circulated nationally in the *Police Gazette*, a publication specifically for police officers but also to help trace suspects, witnesses and, in this case, property. It was further circulated by police forces to jewellers or other businesses that may provide further evidence. Sure enough, on the afternoon of 8 November 1952, two men were spotted outside a jeweller's shop in Bedford High Street. One of the men entered the shop and asked the manager if he could make some repairs to the outer case of a pocket-watch. These were carried out and the man took the watch and duly left the shop. Outside he handed the watch to the other man, who examined it. Then the first customer re-entered the shop and asked if the numerals on the watch face could be repainted. The manager advised him of the difficulties of such work and again the man left the shop. On this occasion both men left the area of the shop front and never returned. Dutifully, the manager notified the police of his suspicions. He described both men as vagrant types, rough and unkempt in appearance, not the sort one would expect to possess a pocket-watch. The sad fact of this incident is that the pocket-watch was never confirmed as the one that once belonged to George Peach and the two men were never traced.

Eventually, on 13 November 1952, the police finally made a breakthrough in the investigation. Detective Constable Lovell of Wellingborough located and identified a small brown-leather flapover-style purse with thonged edges. The purse was found on a grass-covered bank on the left-hand side of the road running out of the village towards the Polebrook Road. It was close to the garden wall that fronted the home of John Dockray. This was about 800 yards from the scene of the crime and around 125 yards from where the murder weapon had been found. The purse contained a single threepenny piece and, it was believed, had been thrown there by some unknown individual leaving the village. This object was later identified as belonging to Lillian Peach!

It seems quite incredible, as thorough as the police search seems to have been (and certainly photographs of the search team indicate a solid wall of eagle-eyed officers), that two hard-to-ignore key pieces of evidence had been missed during the wave of searches. Having walked the search route myself many times and stood at the precise spot where the purse was found, it would seem impossible for it not to have been seen. Similarly with the coal hammer, the garden where this was found was well kept. How could it simply have found its way 'under' a pile of fallen cabbage leaves so quickly? It would be easy to condemn searching police officers for failing in their duty and responsibility. However, I believe that the fault was not theirs. It would be over-generous to completely exonerate them of all blame, since there is a miniscule chance they did twice fail to identify vital evidence. Yet what if the purse or the coal hammer had not been where they were eventually found during the police search? What if, as seems more than likely, they had been deposited there later, to put the police off the scent of the real killer? Having spoken to some of the officers involved in the investigation, there seems to have been a real belief at the time that evidence was placed after the police search.

Another fact that concerned the police was that there was no

The garden where the murder weapon was found.

suggestion of rogue vehicle tyre-tracks leading up to the cottage. Those that were present were easily identifiable as local traffic. Some bicycle tracks were located close to the cottage but these were dismissed as those from a cycle belonging to William Underwood, a 65-year-old night watchman who was quickly eliminated from the inquiries. Underwood, in fact, provided some extra information that proved useful in the bigger picture of the investigation. He had passed West Lodge at about 10.00 p.m. on the night of 24 October; he had seen no sign of any lights in the house. Further to this, the estate chauffeur, Christopher, confirmed that he passed by West Lodge at around 11.00 p.m. the same night and again there had been no lights on.

The press were, by now, desperate for a story of any sort relating to Ashton. One newspaper informed its readership that the police had in fact cut down the number of suspects to five men. Another ran the headline, 'Is Northants Couple's Murderer Living in Locality?' It was all scurrilous rumour-mongering, suggested in the hope that someone, either from the police, or perhaps a witness, would come forward and speak to them. Eventually the gathered hacks got the quote they had waited for; in essence it proved to be a catastrophic blunder, one which would seriously hamper the entire investigation.

Superintendent Tarr was quoted as saying, 'The murder may have been committed by someone living locally as there was no definite proof to the contrary.' That was it. Suddenly it seemed to the community of Ashton that they were, in fact, all suspects. Worse was to follow. Some enterprising journalist found a local person to say that they were in fear that the killer was still walking among them, as part of their tight-knit community. The entire village turned mute and were, deliberately, one feels, unhelpful to the Scotland Yard detectives' inquiries. For the first time ever, families in Ashton ensured that all their windows and back doors were locked before they went to bed. In some cases, mistrust of the next-door neighbour was evident and a reticence to be open about anything prevailed.

The police managed to track every local man's movements on the night in question, and most had genuine alibis. Three men, estate workers, had returned to the village from London in a lorry at about 12.30 a.m. on the morning of the murder. One was dropped in the village centre, the other two parked up the vehicle and ensured loose cattle were secured in their pens. They had then walked slowly back into the village to their homes. One of the men was Francis Mahoney, who had only lived in Ashton for about four months, having moved there from a similar position in Herefordshire. It seems from all accounts and evidence that Mahoney was indeed the last person out and about in Ashton that evening. He bid his colleague a good night and had to walk a little further to his home. Mahoney and his colleague were spoken to by detectives, and neither recalled seeing or hearing anyone else or any strangers in the village at that time.

The bodies of George and Lillian Peach were buried in the graveyard of Fotheringhay church. Hundreds of mourners attended and a special bus was provided to shuttle the residents of Ashton to the service to pay their last respects.

Scotland Yard were making little or no headway in the case since the public comments made by Superintendent Tarr. So the detectives from the metropolis packed their bags and went home, having done little to aid the ongoing investigation. To be fair, they had met with some resistance locally. However, the Ashton case will forever be one that

Scotland Yard failed to resolve.

As has been discussed here, a number of errors had been made during the initial inquiries under the guidance of Scotland Yard officers. These erroneous judgments undoubtedly worked against the investigating authorities.

Add to this the complex financial implications and the responsibility of a full-blown murder inquiry such as this, and one can begin to see what a heavy burden such matters are on the respective police force. In this instance the local constabulary simply could not afford to maintain the high number of officers it had on the ground in the vicinity of Ashton, and inquiries were unproductive. Local people wanted to put the dreadful memory of the case behind them and move on, hence on Scotland Yard's departure, the investigation was slowly wound

The form distributed by police to the residents of Ashton.

down, with a token few officers being allocated to the investigation, but it was to all intents and purposes a murder investigation now doomed to failure.

Thus for so long things remained unchanged. The residents of Ashton got on with their lives, the police received the occasional communication from people who felt they owned vital evidence, but nothing truly substantial was forthcoming until 4 October 1956 when Scotland Yard detectives received an anonymous call that someone at a fairground in Tottenham was talking quite a lot about an unsolved murder in Northamptonshire that happened four years earlier. The police swooped and eighty men were spoken to and fingerprinted. It was also recalled that a similar funfair had been in Wellingborough at the time of the Ashton murder. The Tottenham funfair yielded no new

Picturesque Fotheringhay Church, where the victims are buried.

The victims' graves.

clues or evidence. All those interviewed were released without any further action. The individual discussing the crime was never traced and was not, it seemed, among this group of fairground people.

Then, in 1990, while researching a book, I began my own inquiries into the case, gaining access to the official police files and tracking down people from the era who lived in the area at the time and had some knowledge of it all. I interviewed many, but many others didn't want to be interviewed and refused to discuss it any further. An anonymous telephone call to a local journalist as a result of my book, which covered, among others, the Ashton case, revealed another potential suspect. In a flurry of headlines it was announced that Northamptonshire police were reviewing the case. The result was another dead end: there was nothing to substantiate the theory proposed to the journalist.

My own research and assessment led me to a very different conclusion about matters. I wrote to (at the time) Lady Miriam Lane asking to interview her about the case. Surprisingly, she responded but asked me to put in writing my own perceptions gleaned from the police file and my own research, which I did. The response I received to this was most surprising. Indeed, Lady Miriam Lane identified to me, in writing, a man whom she claimed had been suspect number one at the time. I shall refer to this suspect simply as 'J' from this point.

So, for the record, this is my own theory on why George and Lillian Peach were killed that evening. There is evidence in the police files that indicates that some of the estate cattle were being sold off on the black market. George Peach, it appears, had inadvertently come across some bottles of poison kept in one of the farm barns or outhouses where some of the cattle were stored. When he questioned why this was there

Old murder —new probe

A picture of Mr. Harry Peach taken some years ago at Peterborough Show.

POLICE SWOOP

SCOTLAND YARD officers have resumed inquiries into the double tragedy which occurred at Ashton, near Oundle on the night of October 25, 1952, when Mr. and Mrs. George Henry Peach were battered to death in their lonely cottage.

The inquiries took on a dramatic turn on Thursday night when, following an anonymous telephone call to the Yard, police officers swooped on a fairground at Tottenham where fingerprints were taken from a large number of fairground workers.

The telephone call from someone in London suggested that police visit the fairground. The call did not refer directly to the Ashton double muder but sufficient information was given to connect the call with it. So far the Yard have been unable to trace who made the call.

Police officers cordoned the fair on Tottenham Marshes while fingerprint experts went to work.

Supt. W. A. Roche, of Wellingborough, and Chief Detective Inspector F. Meacock who were both involved in

Although the fair at Tottenham has never visited this area as a unit, it is appreciated that fairground workers change jobs quite frequently.

Mr. Henry Thurston, well-known Northamptonshire showman who several years ago retired and is now living in Wellingborough said that the fairs which visited Wellingborough travelled only as far south as Cambridgeshire, Tottenham fair was served by the London circuit.

The cottage is now occupied by Mr. and Mrs. Horace Dexter who with their six children have lived there for nearly two years.

Not worried

Shown a report of re-opening of inquiries, Mrs. Dexter said: "I thought it was all finished with. I never thought it would come up again after all this time."

Newspaper coverage of the Peaches' murder. Evening Telegraph he was told it was used solely for medicinal purposes.

Slowly a number of the cattle fell ill and for the formal records had to be destroyed. I believe that in all probability these cattle were not destroyed but sold on the black market. The poison was probably administered in small doses, so as to make the cattle ill, giving them the appearance of dying stock, so authority was given to destroy them.

On the night in question it is claimed that George Peach made mention to a fellow-worker of some 'goings-on' which he disagreed with and intended to speak to Captain Lane about the following day. He never got to make that complaint and was killed before he let the cat out of the bag.

'J' could well have been one of the two cowmen who returned from London on the morning of the murder. Certainly, the day after the crime, the suspect applied for another similar job in the North of England; this in my opinion was most sinister. It was no coincidence that J's wife was the sole witness who claimed to hear a 'rogue' vehicle entering the village between 1.00 a.m. and 2.00 a.m. after her husband was of course safely wrapped up in bed. There was no evidence of rogue vehicle tracks other than those successfully traced by the police.

'J' had all the time and opportunity to go to West Lodge, commit the crime and return hitherto unhindered or without arousing any suspicion whatsoever. After all, he had the perfect alibi: he was meant to be out late having just returned from London. There is clear evidence that the killer must have known his way round the inside of the house: he climbed in through a rear pantry window that was filled with possible obstructions. 'J' lived in a similar house in the village, though his was not a detached property. He entered with the coal hammer in his possession with a view to using it on George Peach to silence him. The taking of the hammer into the house by the suspect is an important point. It indicates a premeditated aggravated attack. A common burglar, on the other hand, would have been unarmed and would have preferred to remain in the downstairs rooms rather than gamble on going upstairs and being detected.

We know that the killer made his way up the stairs to the first floor. He was looking for George, and soon found him and duly killed him, locking the bedroom door on his way out of the room to delay the finding of the body. Lillian heard the commotion and was duly attacked by the suspect, as she at once recognised him and so had to be silenced too. To cover his tracks, and in an attempt to give the appearance of a burglary, the suspect then took a few objects from the house, including cash, a watch, a purse and a jewellery trinket drawer from a cabinet in Lillian's room, and left via the front door of the house.

The key to the bedroom door was probably discarded well away from the scene of the crime and the murder weapon hidden, then later deposited in Mrs Marsh's garden after the police search.

If this theory and my conclusions all sound too neat and tidy then that is because they are accurate. On researching 'J' I identified that a similar crime occurred where he previously worked. Certainly Lady Miriam Lane believed this man to be suspect number one; she told me so in a signed, handwritten letter she sent to me in 1990. The police themselves clearly held a belief that the killer was a local man. I believe 'J' was that man. He lived in the village and was part of the community. Other factors I could introduce into this scenario include the finding of the purse belonging to Lillian Peach. This was found not too far from his home, albeit at sufficient distance for it not to be at once associated with him. Similarly with the bloodstained coal hammer – the murder weapon – this too was found within a few yards of his home.

The police were foiled in their efforts to procure evidence to support the black-market sale of cattle. Once this had been established as a potential motive the officers from Scotland Yard were removed from the investigation. The local police, on the other hand, were forced to wind down the inquiry and suddenly, the murder of George and Lillian Peach became an unsolved mystery; a mystery which contains so many red herrings and complications as to make the case of Jack the Ripper look rather straightforward.

The mystery and intrigue of this case somewhat overshadow the tragic end which fell to the lives of George and Lillian Peach and the heartache felt by their family, all because of selfish greed.

Select Bibliography

Bedford Prison Archives, A.A. Rouse

Critchley, T.A., *A History of Police in England and Wales* (1979)

Curtis, Evelyn, *Crime in Bedfordshire 1660-1688*

Gould, Jack, *Gothick Northamptonshire* (1992)

Harrison, Paul, *Jack the Ripper – The Mystery Solved* (1991)

Harrison, Paul, *Northamptonshire Murders*, (1991)

Hibbert, Christopher, *The Roots of Evil; A Social History of Crime and Punishment* (1966)

Hopkins, Matthew, *The Discovery of Witches* (1647)

Knapp, Andrew and Baldwin, William, *The Newgate Calendar* (1826)

Lane, Brian, The Murder Club Guide to the Midlands (1988)

Markham, Christopher, *Ancient Punishments in Northamptonshire* (1886)

Normanton, Helena, Trial of A.A. Rouse (1931)

Northamptonshire Notes and Queries

Northamptonshire Police Museum papers including,

    Official Police Investigation file, Alfred Arthur Rouse

    Official Police Investigation file, Ashton Murders

Pelham, Camden, *Chronicles of Crime* (1841)

Pipe, Marian, booklets:

    Ghosts and Folklore of Northamptonshire (1986)

    Legends of Northamptonshire (1984)

    Mysteries and Memorials of Northamptonshire (1988)

    Myths and Legends of Northamptonshire (1985)

Stearne, John, *A Confirmation and Discovery of Witchcraft* (1648)

Kettering Evening Telegraph

Northampton Herald

Northampton Mercury

Index